DEVELOP EXPONENTIAL POWER

Everything you know about
POWER is WRONG!!!

A NEW GUIDE AND THEORY TO
ACHIEVEMENT BEYOND YOUR
WILDEST DREAMS

BJORN CHRISTIAN MARTINOFF
Foreword by Roland Sullivan

Develop Exponential Power

More Praise for

Develop Exponential Power

Dear Bjorn,

I believe I owe you my sincerest feedback. It may be noteworthy to indicate on the front cover that your book is an indispensable guide to executives, leaders, and aspiring leaders alike, including anyone who wants to truly succeed in business, politics, and life in general.

Your book is so moving, timely, and personal. It bridges and harmonizes all kinds of relationships. It encourages deep reflection in order for one to recognize a precious gift in all of us – the power of discernment. The lessons you teach can be applied in any setting. The exercises are realistic. I can tell that your book will definitely touch many lives and so I'd like to thank you personally for opening my own soul.

Reading your book was like watching my life unfold. You made me realize that I've always had the power in me to impact many lives but I only needed to be told. Exponential Power is truly achievable with a strong will.

Thank you again for the privilege you have given me to have a preview. I wish you more blessings, Bjorn, so that you may continue to be a blessing to others too.

Regards,
Michelle Lucas, CEO

Develop Exponential Power

Dear Bjorn,

Hope this mail finds you well and you had a good trip to India.

I had a chance to read your book in snatches, and am looking forward to being able to settle down to a full read some time soon. The plan is to buy a hard copy, have it autographed by you, and savor it chapter by chapter.

What I have read, I have enjoyed thoroughly. I enjoy the style, which is simple and yet conveys the message powerfully. What I enjoy even more are the different aspects of value-driven leadership and serving them as an integrated whole, leading to exponential returns.

I feel so proud to know you. What you have accomplished is really awesome. I use the much mouthed word "awesome" in all its former glory.

Warm regards,
 Smriti Ahuja, Consultant, Coca-Cola

Develop Exponential Power

Dear Bjorn,

WOW, I am impressed!! Had a skim through the pages and what pops very quickly is how easy and very consistent it is to read. There is a pattern that helps the audience to quickly grasp what the book will give them. There's a very good "catch line" which will draw them into the details further, not to mention the exercises which later on I found out actually are more of a practical way of helping the reader find the sources in which they can cultivate these values or qualities.

Your book is a very easy to follow and read, filled with lots of positive ideas and practical examples. I also like the fact that one can basically jump directly into the subjects that tickles one's interest without missing the idea. If anything, one can easily go back and forth and build on the different ideas and connect them to make an even stronger synergy between them.

Warmest,
Sri Widowati, L'Oreal

"I highly recommend this book, I couldn't put it down, and it's like Sun Tzu's Art of War, in business approach."
Johnny Michael Robledo, Student of Life

Develop Exponential Power

Dear Bjorn,

I just finished reading your new publication and I wanted to start off by saying thank you. It has been a privilege for me to read this! I enjoyed it so much and I have so many thoughts to share with you that I don't know where to start.

What I loved about your book is that it was indeed easy to read, no fancy pansy theories. Every power you wrote about relates to me, so I am sure it will relate to everyone and anyone who reads it.

I find your book so practical and useful anytime, anywhere.

The book is rather personal. I could hear your voice as I read it, and at times I felt we were having a conversation. There were moments I had something to say about your point and was mumbling to myself, so this was why I felt we were talking. What I missed about your book, especially the preface, is that you hardly mentioned that you were sharing your own personal experiences. I think this is important. The preface was a little theoretical for me. I would rather you just tell me how I can use this book, what it would give me, and that it was written from your heart and based on your experience. This would be enough for me to buy it.

I learned so much from this read. Firstly, I finally understood what you meant by being authentic. I was not clear in my head, but when I read your chapter on this, I instantly got it. I also enjoyed your chapter on integrity. I always saw it as more about being honest and having a certain "code of ethics". I like your interpretation – much easier, still value-based and achievable for all.

Develop Exponential Power

I can't really say how this book should be improved. I am not an expert. While reading I did like some chapters better than others, but I suppose this is what you wanted it to be like. All in all, I still truly enjoyed reading it. Many of the lessons are stuck in my head and I am already practicing some.

Thank you again. It's a great product, and I admire the work you have put into it. It will be useful to many people.

Congratulations Bjorn – a beautiful piece of work.

Regards,
Jennifer Francis, Asian Development Bank

Develop Exponential Power

"He who controls others may be powerful, but he who has mastered himself is mightier still."

LAO-TZU

Develop
EXPONENTIAL
POWER

Stop Chasing It and Let It Chase You

A NEW GUIDE AND THEORY TO ACHIEVEMENT BEYOND YOUR WILDEST DREAMS

By BJORN MARTINOFF

Copyright Bjorn Martinoff 2013

Develop Exponential Power

Copyright © 2013 by Bjorn C. Martinoff. All rights reserved.

Published by F1C International, Manila, Philippines

No part of this publication may be reproduced, stored in a retrieval system, or transmitted in any form or by any means, electronic, mechanical, photocopying, recording, scanning, or otherwise, except as permitted under Section 107 or 108 of the 1976 United States Copyright Act, without either the prior written permission of the Publisher, or authorization through payment of the appropriate per-copy fee to the Publisher.

Requests to the Publisher for permission should be addressed to the Permissions Department, F1C International, 9719 Pililia Street #201, Makati City, Philippines, 1208, info@fortune100coach.com

Tel.: +632-478-3844

Limit of Liability/Disclaimer of Warranty: While the publisher and author have used their best efforts in preparing this book, they make no representations or warranties with respect to the accuracy or completeness of the contents of this book and specifically disclaim any implied warranties of merchantability or fitness for a particular purpose. No warranty may be created or extended by sales representatives or written sales materials. The advice and strategies contained herein may not be suitable for your situation. You should consult with a professional where appropriate. Neither the publisher not author shall be liable for any loss of profit or any other damages, commercial or otherwise, including but not limited to special, incidental, consequential, or other damages.

Printed in the Philippines.

For my wife Victoria, and my children Minday, Maxwell, Malcolm, and Sarah.

You are my sunshine.

You are my life.

Develop Exponential Power

ACKNOWLEDGMENTS

Rev. Dr. Michael Beckwith says it takes a village to raise a child and I say it takes a village to inspire an author, or at least that's what it seemed to take for me. And so I'd like to thank and acknowledge all of those who have been an inspiration to me.

My special thanks and gratitude go to my wife Victoria and our wonderful children. You are the light of my life. I thank you for your trust and patience, without it this book would not have been possible.

I also like to thank Rev. Dr. Michael Beckwith, Neale Donald Walsch, Marianne Williamson, Anthony Robbins, Werner Erhard, the Forum Leaders of Landmark Education, Lou Tice, and my many other teachers for their wonderful, wonderful inspiration over many years.

I want to thank my many coaches for their great support over the years. They are my dear friends and supporters along the way – Nika Solomon, Cristelle Morrison, Roderick Sun, Harry and Martina Sprangers, Aljor Perreras, Christine Garcia, Angela Chen, Jennifer Francis, Bert and Renilde Demeyere, Smriti Ahuja, Arvy Villamarzo, Sri Widowati, Michelle Lucas, Johnny Michael Robledo, Jerry Perez de Tagle, Darrel Gurney,

Sarah Weston, Barbara Martinoff, Roland Sullivan, Professor Peter Koestenbaum, and many others. You supported me when I was not yet on the map. I thank you.

Thank you also to my wonderful and hardworking editors Eileen Tupaz as and Anthony Alcantara.

Without you this book may have taken a couple more years to complete.

I also like to thank my family especially my Mom Karin and my Dad Marius Martinoff as well as my dear, dear uncle Bjoern B. Martinoff whom I was named after.

Most of all I'd like to thank God, my ever loving and inspiring higher power and friend, for all the loving support when I most needed it and for sending his great Angels in the middle of the night and in the darkest time of my life. Thank you.

FOREWORD

by Roland Sullivan

Hang on to your hat, as you see and feel all around you, a whirlwind of change.

"The Times They Are A-Changin'!" Globalization and technology will change our world beyond what our imagination can now believe. More change and transformation will occur in your lifetime than since the beginning of recorded civilization over 4,500 years ago.

More than ever we all need rock solid principles or fundamental truths to root us in the ever-shifting paradigms. The only constants are our core principles and relationships.

If I were to list my top philosophical golden nuggets, all of Martinoff's would be on the list. They are me... articulated.

The purpose of my writing this foreword is to share with you a resource that will help you become one step closer to heroic greatness.

Develop Exponential Power

In 1962, I was first introduced in a National Training Lab to the world of the change-agent profession. The lab opened my eyes to inner power. Since then I have spent my life doing my best to help individuals (especially executive leaders) and corporations discover their power so they can realize their potential. It is my life's purpose to help leaders empower their people through influence rather than the outdated 'Command and Demand Power' which as Bjorn states is really Force not Power. My large group interactions release uniting power lying dormant in the whole system. I believe that powerful influence with a spirit of free choice is one of the primordial competencies for today. In these changing times, we need leaders to be more powerful than ever before. This is a power that one cannot chase but a power that flows freely from one's inner being. Power: From a majestic bed of intuition to a welcoming, trusting, open, and self-realizing recipient.

In this new and ever-changing, borderless, and flattening world there is nothing more practical than guiding principles to support the kind of results people and organizations desire.

Develop Exponential Power

Therefore, I am honored to introduce you to this fresh take on ancient and golden wisdoms. It is brilliance that transcends epochs.

Here we have for the first time in today's global language, essential mindsets to help refine your "self as an instrument of positive change." This is a great handbook for you to facilitate change with individuals and organizations. These concepts will help you lead them faster, much, much faster, toward the realization and then actualization of excellence.

I am thrilled in both my mind and heart to introduce Bjorn's book that you now are holding in your hands. I first scanned a draft of this book when Bjorn and I first met at the famed Peninsula Hotel in Manila, Philippines. Bjorn and I immediately hit it off because I felt he had eloquently expressed what I felt are the universal theorems needed today and missing in many change efforts. He comprehends who I am. I just have never seen them all so clearly stated together.

Bjorn spells out what my philosophical soul has been wanting to express so clearly and this supports helping leaders today hone the key competencies needed for

Develop Exponential Power

successful leadership.

I felt joyous at the headline of each chapter. Each chapter is so relevant as we move into the "Age of Aquarius", or as I call it the "Age of Transformation." It will be interesting to see how you apply these golden gems to your self, your teams, and your organization.

Allow me to share a few examples that verify the importance that I have them being.

The Power of Trust:

> I did my Ph.D. study under Dr. Jack Gibb. He wrote the first book on trust as it relates to individual and organization development. Jack is one of the 12 disciples of Lewin who coined the phrase "Social Psychology." He was the first to focus on group process, feedback and the prelude to change agents, organization development and transformation. I always start my interventions with an organization assessment. Trust, 90% of the time, becomes a key issue to be addressed.

The Power of Purpose:

> For every small or comprehensive intervention, I start with clarifying purpose.

Develop Exponential Power

The Powers of Vision, Courage and Reality:

> One of my two living mentors is Dr. Peter Koestenbaum. For me he is the number one business philosopher of the last century. He was the first to write about the heart of business. Vision, Courage, and Reality are his key powers. His fourth power is ethics. All of Bjorn's principles assume ethical behavior.

The Powers of Action and Commitment:

> Those who know me well understand that for every executive team or large group transformation that I facilitate, my two main products are actions and commitments. These two stalwarts frame sustainable change for me.

The Power of Presence:

> Full presence is my advice to anyone who is faced with supporting a person who is in a hopeless situation such as a death being eminent. Just be fully attentive and concentrated on who they are and what they are confronting is so loving.

Develop Exponential Power

The Power of Humility:

> A client, John, just received from the CEO the "change agent of the corporation award." This is from one of the world's largest insurance companies. His people have told me that his humble mindset gave him the power to lead change in an extraordinary manner. His excellent performance is powered or fueled by humility.

The Power of Growth:

> Growth for me is a positive change. People who grow are the happiest. My degree in philosophy essentially taught me that human beings' greatest aspiration is to be happy.

The Power of Authenticity:

> When we created the first definition for Asia by Asians of organization development. A key phrase was "authentic leadership."

The Power of Belief:

> My proven theory of transformation is distilled to the powers of reality, vision, action, and belief.

Develop Exponential Power

Oh. My favorite principle is free Choice. I believe the most important gift that life has given us is that of free will. Our divine given free will is the steering wheel for our inner power. We make countless choices each day. Each choice either brings us closer to happiness or closer to sadness. We can choose to be vivacious, cheerful, energetic, positive, or even ecstatic. Or the countless choices we make each day can cause sadness, sickness, complacency, being negative, or even depressed.

Helping others brings joy. Hurting our self or others deflates our joy.

It is up to you! It is your choice!

Do you want to become happier or end your life a grumpy old person in poverty and depression. The sky is the limit for your joy. These principles show the way.

It is up to you. Choose to be so that power and goodness come to you.

My wish is that you use this book to help you choose greatness. I want you to be or become a powerful super hero helping the world become one in the spirit of love, all while you become prosperous materially and spiritually.

Develop Exponential Power

So you can see the principles presented here align with my passion of helping all be and become GREAT! This book leaves you with the practical tools for your internal change efforts and its sustainability.

There is something in you that made you pick up "Develop Exponential Power: Stop Chasing It and Let It Chase You". The moment you laid your eyes on this and chose to pick it up, you knew that this book is for you. Notice there's a spark of greatness within you that is already unleashed.

Wherever you are on the globe and in the game of your life, you have your own vast territory to master. This master book provides you the space for your wildfire of success.

Allow me to share how I am applying the gems in this book in my life. Each Sunday, I start my day by reading just one chapter. I then still my mind for an hour and watch all the wonderful ideas float into my empty mind that I can utilize in the next week. With my iPhone, I dictate using Dragon Dictate the great and powerful ideas that flew into my quiet, relaxed yet concentrated mind. I print out my thoughts. Mostly there are actions and commitments. I post them next to my desk. I notice them many times a day. I am just amazed how many times during the week I use Bjorn's truths to frame my behavior. Often they surface as reminders as I work with my clients.

"Develop Exponential Power" has become a modern day bible for me. It has been nutrition for my soul and a driving force for my work as a driver of change!

You now hold the guide and wisdom to achievement beyond your wildest dreams.

Here's to wielding your own power!

I highly recommend this book, I can't give any higher recommendation than this. As I said above, this book is me ... articulated.

About Roland Sullivan

Roland is one of the original 100 change agents and likely one of the top two or three at the moment. He learned directly from the founders of the field since 1962. He has led change efforts in over 1,000 organizations in 35 countries. He has taught OD at 12 universities, including Pepperdine which has the most recognized change program in the world.

Editing 20+ change books, including the popular third edition of Practicing Organization Development, has kept him on the cutti ng edge of global best practices. He is best known for "actually" transforming whole systems in large interactive events.

For over two decades, Roland has served as Chair of the OD Institute's Committee to Define Knowledge and Skills for Competence in OD. The Institute uses this research in accrediting university programs around the globe in organization change.

In 2004, he cofounded the Asian OD Network.

He has Master's degrees in Organization Development from Loyola in Chicago and Pepperdine in Los Angeles. Pepperdine is reputed to have the most recognized global degree on managing change in the world.

Both the American Society of Training and Development as well as the Minnesota OD Network granted him their Organization Development Professional of the Year awards.

Develop Exponential Power

CONTENTS

More Praise_____3
Acknowledgements _____13
Foreword _____15
Contents_____25
Preface _____29
Introduction_____39

    The Power of ACTION_____41
    How to tell which actions are most fulfilling

    The Power of ALIGNMENT_____49
    How to triple your results without any extra effort

    The Power of AUTHENTICITY_____63
    How to cut through the smoke screen and get to the bottom line

    The Power of BELIEF_____71
    How what you believe can bring you to a screeching halt

    The Power of CHOICE_____77
    How to have a choice even when there isn't any

    The Power of COMMITMENT_____83
    The driving power behind your goals

    The Power of CONTRIBUTION_____89
    Be energized by making a difference

    The Power of COURAGE_____97
    Expand then blow apart your limits

    The Power of DETACHMENT_____105
    Being open to something most often brings it

Develop Exponential Power

The Power of EMPATHY _____ 119
How to have instant access to someone's world

The Power of FAITH _____ 125
How to have certainty in uncertain times

The Power of FLEXIBILITY _____ 131
Getting what you want even when there are obstacles

The Power of FOCUS _____ 139
Your road sign to your destiny

The Power of FUN _____ 145
How to have more energy when you need it most

The Power of GRATITUDE _____ 149
What if being thankful is paying it forward?

The Power of GROWTH _____ 155
How to accelerate your growth and supercharge your success

The Power of HUMILITY _____ 161
How being powerful and humble makes you unforgettable

The Power of INSPIRATION _____ 167
Self-motivate when it's needed most

The Power of INTEGRITY _____ 175
Without it nothing works

The Power of INTERPRETATION _____ 181
How to turn lead into gold

Develop Exponential Power

The Power of LUCK _____ 187
How to have more and on demand

The Power of PEACE _____ 193
The stability that brings about momentum

The Power of PRESENCE _____ 199
How to nurture it as a gift to others

The Power of PURPOSE _____ 207
Driven by WHY

The Power of REALITY _____ 217
Knowing where you are will tell you the directions

The Power of RESPONSIBILITY _____ 223
Victim or victor? The choice is yours

The Power of TRUST _____ 229
Opening doors the gentle way

The Power of VISION _____ 235
How being clear about what you want attracts it

THE POWERS IN BRIEF _____ 239
WHAT'S NEXT _____ 242
SOME BOOK RECOMMENDATIONS _____ 244
ABOUT THE AUTHOR _____ 245
CONTACT BJORN MARTINOFF _____ 246

Develop Exponential Power

PREFACE

At the everyday level of conversation and understanding, power has gotten a bad rap. It has often been confused with force, manipulation, or worse. This deserves clarification. Power in our context deserves to be redeemed and refers in this writing to our ability to influence ourselves primarily, and our environment and the behavior of other people secondarily. Basically it's about getting things done. Hundreds of books have been written on the subject—books whose success in the market testifies to a deeply felt need we all have to gain or develop in ourselves. While Power is often confused with force and manipulation, it is only true power, inner power, the power to control ourselves along with the appropriate beingness that truly enlivens and inspires others. True power therefore is not given or taken or manipulated. True power is lived, exuded from within, demonstrated, and shared. For power to be expressed outwardly we need to consider three important realms that are ACTIONS, SYSTEMS, and PARADIGMS. Actions or tasks are self-explanatory and so are systems as they are structures by which we operate and get things done. By Paradigms we mean ways of thinking, ways of being which is also known as a beingness or beingnesses, and include values and beliefs.

Develop Exponential Power

This book does not aim to be complete, nor all encompassing, and its intent is to focus on the beingnesses required to achieve exponential power. This we see as essential if not most important about acquiring power.

While other books offer invaluable insights on getting things done your way, they tend to emphasize scenarios whose applications are often limited to complicated schemes of manipulation.

True power is not force by imposing one's will on another, nor is it manipulation because at the heart of manipulation lies an admission that you may not be powerful enough and therefore need to deploy some sort of farce, force, or make-believe scenario that fools others into compliance or into playing a hand less advantageous to them. While these tactics may get a result, they are much less satisfying in the end even if we win with them because in our hearts we will always know that we only "won" because we tricked the other. While these tactics can fool others at times they never fool ourselves into believing that true power resides in us.

For instance, many, many others focus on the general techniques that usually enhance it (such as promoting oneself, building networks, and cultivating an image). And in many cases across the board, power tends to be used synonymously with force—a tool that somehow seems to involve and necessitate persuasion, manipulation, and even deception and outright warfare.

Develop Exponential Power

Why the effectiveness of such principles mentioned in the previous paragraph can be limited is because: (1) they foster the view that power is dependent on having a certain title, or position of influence, or being in a particular situation; (2) they presume that people can remember and apply at the right moment *all* the hundreds and thousands of tips and techniques that grant or maximize what they call power in various situations; and (3) by confusing power with force, they leave an impression that power is somehow inherently evil—an immoral capacity that we have to exercise simply to get our way or because so much in our lives depends on it.

This book is based on an entirely different premise. It proceeds from my observations that:

1. Access to power is an ability all human beings have.

2. This ability can be developed to extraordinary degrees by cultivating habitual ways of being rather than by memorizing routine ways of doing.

3. It is an ability that doesn't carry the negative connotations of force because it *is* distinct from force.

Force is the "push" against resistance in order to make things happen, while power eludes resistance by using the "pull" of attraction, inspiration, alignment, and partnership.

Develop Exponential Power

In other words, we already possess a certain amount of power and we can develop it to any degree that we desire. Furthermore, it's an ability that doesn't necessarily involve any of the negative practices that are said to go with it: practices such as persuasion, manipulation, and deception.

What this book therefore describes are the fundamental bases of power—ways of being in the world that generate power as a by-product rather than as a function of personality, circumstance, or strategy. Ways of being transcend personality, are indifferent to circumstance, and ultimately underlie all strategy. They can therefore be applied by anyone at any time, place, and situation without the usual constraint of having to act or behave in certain ways.

Having to act or behave in certain ways falls under the domain of following "laws." Because people usually relate to power as the result of acting or behaving in particular ways, books about power often talk about the "laws" of power. But laws exist only when, and because, people don't live by a common set of values. If people lived by common values, no laws would be needed. The same notion applies to so-called laws of power.

Why I like to view this book as a guide to "exponential power" is because when the ways of being that generate power are practiced together, their cumulative effect is exponential. The ways of being described in this book are already enormously effective when applied individually—but what they provide when they're practiced in combination, rapid succession, or *en masse*

Develop Exponential Power

is an unprecedented shift in your level of personal power that can hardly be grasped by merely reading about it. You will actually have to practice it to get a full grasp and understanding of the inner power that is about to be revealed to you.

The following graphics will illustrate that frequent and continuous shifts in beingness/values are inherently exponential.

Graphic 1.1 – Normal Growth:

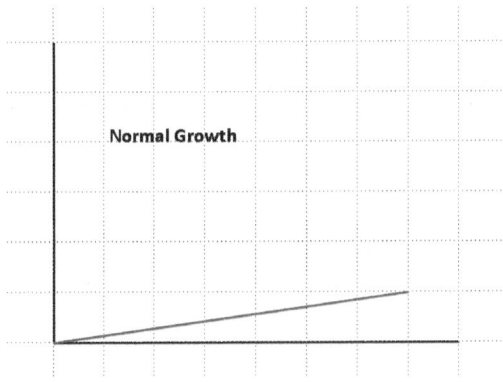

This is roughly what we would expect to see in normal growth, a steady incline with some minor ups and downs in most cases.

Graphic 2.1 – Growth through upgraded skills:

Develop Exponential Power

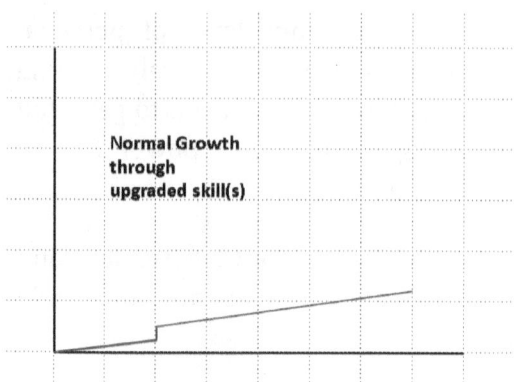

There is a small but nearly immediate impact of upgraded skills, but when observed further this doesn't translate into a trajectory at a steeper angle. It does however translate into continued normal growth at a slighly higher level.

Graphic 3.1 – Growth after Life Changing Impact

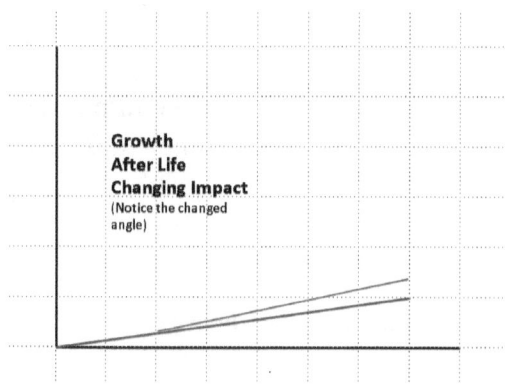

Here the angle, or call it trajectory, has now taken on a new direction which over time will make a major difference. While in the beginning the impact may occur

Develop Exponential Power

as small, the impact over time becomes greater and greater compared with the original "normal" growth trajectory in graphic 1.1 and becomes quite large in time.

Graphic 4.1 – Exponential Power and Growth As a Result of repeated Life Changes in Being.

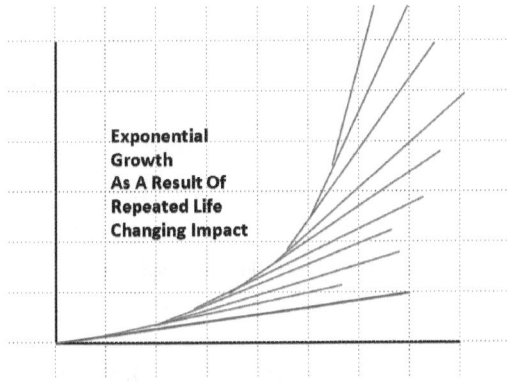

What is shown here is the impact on the growth of the learner after frequently repeated life changing shifts in beingness.

Graphic 5.1 Exponential Growth means Radical Results

Develop Exponential Power

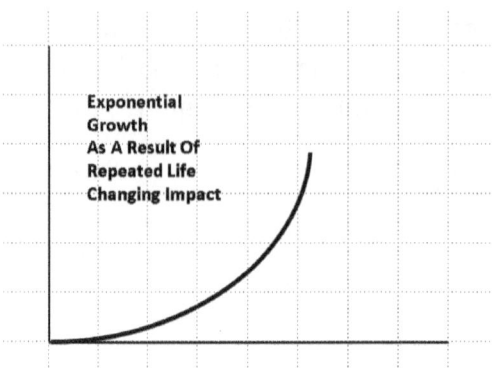

In Graphic 5.1 we have cleaned up the curve. It is now more visible how exponential growth can be made accessible to individuals. However this is not just for individuals, it is also possible for teams and entire organizations.

Is exponential growth unusual? Not in nature. In nature everything grows exponentially. Plants grow exponentially. Exponential growth is not unusual at all. What is unusual really is when we think we can only grow at 4, 5, 6 or 10percent per year, or less.

While I have made all attempts to write in a straightforward language, the content can actually be viewed as a highly advanced conversation. A first step is to understand it.

Each chapter presents the opportunity to change your life in a significant way that can empower you dramatically. Combined, these teachings will help you grow exponentially as you turn each chapter from mere knowledge into action. Because it needs to be put into action, I say knowledge is worthless, but more precisely

Develop Exponential Power

I would say "knowledge that isn't being used is worthless." Knowledge that is being put into action becomes highly valuable.

So take caution - the knowledge you gain here by itself will make no difference. It will however make a BIG difference once you apply the knowledge that you will gain from this book. The difference the application of this knowledge will make is exponential.

True power is accessible to all people independent of backgrounds, levels of education, and motivations—whether they be executives who have likely already read other sources on power or younger people who may never have previously read anything on the subject.

Whatever your background or your motivation may be in reading or examining this book, it is designed to provide you with access to more, much more access to your inner power, AND the ability to live this new power, making it an experience that will leave you touched, moved, and inspired.

May you use this power to become the master of your own destiny—and may you use the influence you subsequently generate wisely and for the good of all mankind.

- *Bjorn Martinoff*

Develop Exponential Power

"In life, understanding is the booby prize."

- WERNER ERHARD

INTRODUCTION

How to read this book

To start with I feel it is important to know that this book includes my personal experiences and a lifetime of learning. Many of the stories in here are experiences that have happened to me personally. As we go along I will be sharing my own experiences straight from my heart.

There really is no right or wrong way to read this book. The way it is structured allows you to choose between reading it straight from front to back, or reading selected chapters as the desire or inspiration arises.

Each chapter is devoted to a way of being that is sufficient in generating power for you in and by itself. Yet when the various principles are *applied together* (in twos, or threes, or even more), they exponentially increase the power that they make available to you.

Rather than relating to these ways of being, however, as yet another set of techniques to memorize, I encourage you to cultivate them as habits instead. The virtue of a habit over a technique is that of an automatic reaction versus a deliberate response, a habit takes far less time and effort to apply in a specific situation. For example, when you get out of bed, you proceed to brush your teeth through sheer force of habit—it is an action that no longer needs the time and effort of deliberate thought or intention.

The work that you have to do while reading this book therefore lies in getting habituated to the ways of being it recommends. One of the most effective ways of accomplishing this habituation is by reading or reviewing a chapter for a day (or a week) and then repeatedly performing its suggested exercise throughout the day (or the week).

At some point, the way of being will become a reflexive response, and generating power will become increasingly easier. It can certainly not be easy at the start (in the same way that brushing your teeth first thing in the morning may not have been easy at the start), but I promise you that the effort is worth it (as the current healthy state of your gums has proven).

Just a final word on applying the ways of being suggested in this book: take the principles that work for you and *only* the principles that work for you. Yet in order for you to determine which principles work for you or not, you have to test them thoroughly *at least once*. So proceed as a scientist would—with a spirit of genuine curiosity as to what will ultimately prove effective. You will not only discover things that may surprise you, but you will expand your capacity to generate power and results in your endeavors. And it's this, and only this, that is the intention of this book.

Develop Exponential Power

The Power of

ACTION

"Massive consistent action with pure persistence and a sense of flexibility in pursuing your goals will ultimately give you what you want."

— ANTHONY ROBBINS

In life, there's only one way to generate any kind of result, and that's by taking action. The result you get depends on the kind of action you take. In general, there are three kinds of action: actions that create, actions that maintain, and actions that destroy.

Actions that destroy are pretty straightforward. Where people are getting confused is when it comes to actions that create and actions that maintain.

Very often, people spend their time and energy taking action to maintain something. They'll water the plants daily to maintain their garden, go to the gym weekly to maintain their health, and visit their mothers monthly to maintain their relationship. What people don't realize, however, is that taking action to merely maintain something usually isn't very inspiring. In fact, it often ends up being work.

That's why I assert that it's vitally important to keep our actions in the realm of creation. No matter how small an action might be, it's important to have it *create* something versus just keeping something alive.

If you look back in your life, you'll understand what I'm talking about. Have you noticed, for instance, that you're always most excited and most enthusiastic at the beginning of a project? It's like you're brimming with time, energy and ideas, and the results usually come fast. That's the power of creation as opposed to the power of preservation.

One good example in 2012 is the court battle between Apple and Samsung. While Apple has done very well for itself Samsung seems to have been out-innovating Apple in terms of hardware. With Samsung having come out with many different hardware designs compared to Apple's few, it is not hard to understand why Apple has felt threatened and gone into a defensive and preservationist mode. But suing Samsung is not what will keep Apple at the forefront. The only way Apple will stay there is by remaining on the cutting edge of innovation.

The metaphor of a race car may be helpful here. In a car race you wouldn't win the race by putting on the brakes of your competitor's car. I have actually witnessed something like this in a motocross race. Some competitors will actually move next to another rider and apply their brakes. The trouble with that is a) you wouldn't feel good about winning, IF you did. And b) in order to keep hitting your competitor's brakes you'll actually find yourself remaining right next to him. In the meantime while you're busy battling one, another one may pass you by and actually win that race.

The only way to win is by out-accelerating your competition. The need for both competitors is to create new products that consumers want. So far both Apple and Samsung are doing well and given Samsung's speed in hardware innovation it will be a race to watch for sure. I know Apple must be feeling the pressure.

But how, you ask, can you stay in the realm of creation without having to come up with new projects all the time? In fact, isn't it kind of fickle and irresponsible to keep coming up with new things?

Here's my answer: creating something *new* doesn't necessarily mean creating a new *project*. In fact, you can always create something new even with old or existing projects. It's the freshness and novelty that you inject into these projects by creating something new that keeps you in the realm of excitement and inspiration.

For example, let's say that one project you have in your life is to cook your own meals so that you can control your nutritional intake better. Like any new project, this will excite you a lot in the beginning. But after days and weeks of taking the time and attention that's needed to prepare healthy food, this project will start becoming a *chore*—a clear sign that the actions have devolved to a level of maintenance. In the beginning it was new and

Develop Exponential Power

exciting; it was a new future being created. Much like the work of a leader, once that future has been established it becomes the work of a manager to maintain it. Once you have tasted the excitement of being a leader it may not be nearly as exciting to be managing and maintaining it. There is juice, power, excitement, and energy in continuously creating.

Actions that can bring a project back into the realm of creation can be: (1) making improvements to your product, service, or simply preparing a week's worth of meals without repeating a single dish; (2) preparing products/meals just as good/healthy but at half the price; or (3) creating new audiences and customers by convincing someone else to eat healthily just by having them taste how good your dishes are!

The point is, in each of the actions I just gave as an example, something new was added to the project that wasn't there before—a new dimension or a new context that can provide a fresh source of motivation and inspiration. This is what I mean when I say that you can always keep your actions in the realm of creation without having to create new projects all the time.

Another fairly recent example of maintaining versus creation was the appointment of an outsider to head a Japanese electronics firm. The outsider had been successful in another part of the business but didn't have the passion, inspiration, vision, or leadership to take the spirit of the founders and elevate the electronics business to the next level. The actions he took, actions like laying off people, were meant to help

Develop Exponential Power

but ended up being destructive in nature, even though they were meant to help the company "survive." Yet just because it survived it didn't mean it would thrive. He simply was managing the company while he should have been leading. He was being a manager while what was needed was a leader.

If a company were a race car team managing and fixing the parts that are broken, not bad, but the competition in the meantime may create an entirely new breakthrough racecar.

In my own life, one example of an action I take in the realm of maintenance is to stay in touch with my clients even when my work or project with them is complete or even when I know that they're not in the space for an engagement. This of course only results in a small amount of repeat business. An action that would be in the realm of creation would be to continue to support them, whether paid or not, until such time when we can begin a new project.

Continued assistance could get me more present to new challenges that my clients may be dealing with, which, in turn, could give me ideas on new ways that I can be of service. The same clients may or may not engage me for these services, but other potential clients might. This is an example of being able to continuously generate something new from something that already exists.

Develop Exponential Power

> *"Innovation is a new combination of already existing elements."*
>
> *- BJORN MARTINOFF*

And just by doing this—by taking actions that *create* something new rather than just *maintain* the status quo—we can get enormous power. Power comes naturally in the realm of creation, so an effective way of generating power fast is to simply access this realm.

EXERCISE

Find an area of your life where you're doing things just to maintain the status quo. It could be in the area of your health, the area of your relationships, or the area of your career. It's an area where your time and energy is spent on just keeping things the way they are. For instance, you work out so you don't gain weight, or you take your wife out on dates so she doesn't get upset, or you produce just enough results at work so you get reasonably paid and promoted.

Then in the area you've chosen, take an action that creates something *new*. Run or dance instead of going to the gym. Do something silly with your wife. Ask for a

Develop Exponential Power

project in your office that's totally foreign to you. The point is: Do what it takes to put yourself in the realm of creation rather than in the realm of preservation.

And it's easy to tell when you're in the realm of creation, because the moment you're there, you start feeling excited, you start feeling motivated, and you start feeling inspired. In short: you start feeling powerful.

"The future depends on what we do in the present."

MAHATMA GANDHI

Develop Exponential Power

Develop Exponential Power

The Power of ALIGNMENT

"Just as your car runs more smoothly and requires less energy to go faster and farther when the wheels are in perfect alignment, you and your team perform better when your thoughts, feelings, emotions, goals, actions, and values are in alignment with where you're heading."

- BJORN MARTINOFF

In my experience working with different companies from all over the world—partnering with individual executives of small companies, large companies, struggling companies, Fortune 100 companies, or even the world's largest company—I've found that one of the biggest things that get in the way of their success is the absence of alignment. The absence of alignment is one of the greatest detractors from power being applied toward the desired goal.

Develop Exponential Power

Alignment is critical in any organization because without broad-based agreement, on goals, strategies, and other critical areas, organizations can literally spend a LOT of energy without getting anywhere.

Why?

Well, imagine sitting on a boat with two people rowing: one person is rowing in one direction and the other person is rowing in the opposite direction. If they're both putting in the same amount of energy, they'll just end up canceling each other's efforts and the boat won't move from its location. Or, if one person is putting in more energy than the other, the boat will move in his or her direction, but at a much slower pace than they should be getting with the amount of effort they're exerting.

Now imagine this scenario replicated hundreds of times over in the average-sized organization. In the absence of alignment, there's either no progress at all, or the progress is severely hindered, or it might be severely limited AND going in a different direction than intended.

With alignment, on the other hand, all the individual energies add up and result in a huge amount of momentum. So in cases where a company has clearly established its purpose, its goals, values, and its strategies—and theoretically they're sound—but the company isn't going anywhere, one fruitful area to examine is whether the organization has worked on getting broad-based consensus for its plans.

Develop Exponential Power

I have worked with many outsourcing companies (BPOs). There was one particular company in Asia that has just been warned by its client in the United States that they were at risk of losing their $11,000,000 account. Let's spell that out. It's eleven million dollars. At the moment I learned about this, the business unit ranked last among its network of peers. The client had given it just *two months* to turn the situation around. If not, the the client would pull out.

When I started my engagement with the company, I quickly realized that even just in terms of handling the crisis, there was *no* alignment among the top management team. The energies of the leaders were dispersed, their ideas mixed and unclear, a way forward was vague and unchartered. Something was left to be discovered which would make a difference but none of the leaders could say what it was.

After launching an initial set of diagnostic tools, one of the first things I did with the management team was to help them find alignment and create, in partnership with them, a common vision, purpose, and set of core values.

This wasn't the only intervention I applied, but creating alignment on this broad level provided the foundation for all the other work I needed to do with the organization. Without alignment in terms of the direction we were heading, everything else would fall on deaf ears. Once alignment was in place, the team went on to become the number *two* performer in their network and the number *one* performer in their country—*in less than two months*. And none of this

Develop Exponential Power

would have been possible without an initial alignment of the individual forces.

"Misaligned or even opposing energies and forces are some of the greatest waste and missed opportunities you'll find in organizations."

- BJORN MARTINOFF

Develop Exponential Power

2.1 VECTOR DYNAMICS

To further demonstrate this, as well as the concept of vector dynamics in leadership, let's look at the following graphics:

Graphic 1:

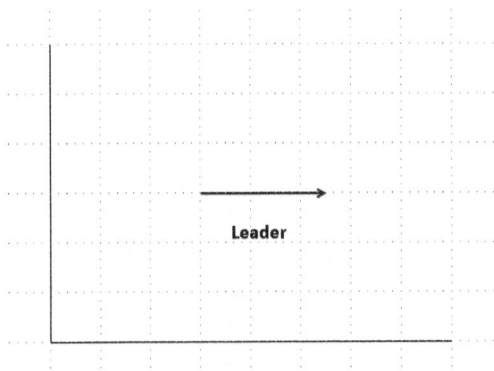

The example in Graphic 1 represents the vector dynamics of a single leader pushing in the direction of her goals or vision. She is a strong leader and pulls forward on a level 2.5. Yet by definition you won't be a leader if you're doing it alone so let's introduce some team members.

Develop Exponential Power

Graphic 2:

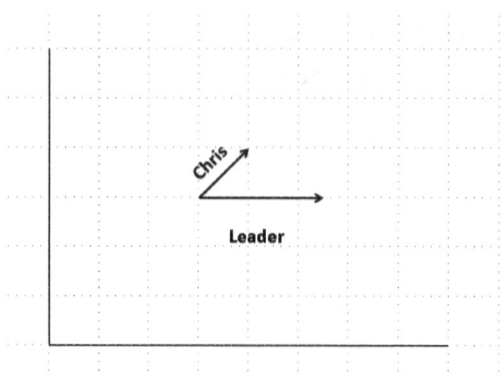

In Graphic 2 Chris is a member of the team. Chris is a professional and appears to be a good team player. Upon further inspection, however, we notice that Chris has some of his own agenda not fully aligned with the Leader. We realize this must have an impact on the combined performance. The question is how much. And that we will see in the following graphics. In the meantime let's add a couple of additonal team members.

Develop Exponential Power

Graphic 3:

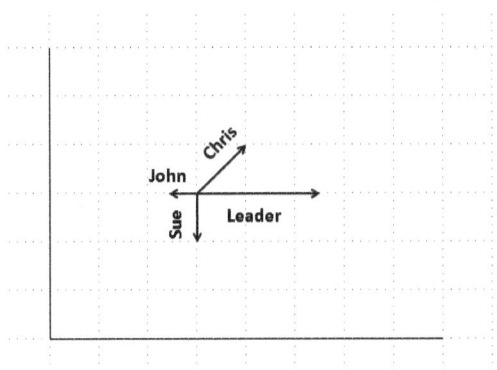

In Graphic 3 we see that our leader now has two additional team members, Sue and John. Sue is in a space where she doesn't really care what she does as long as she brings home a paycheck and is able to pay the bills, while John is mildly upset about being here as he feels it's just a lateral move and he's not inspired by the direction the leader appears to be heading in. In fact John is mildly opposed to where the team seems to be going. Now you may ask yourself what is the outcome or end-effect of the Vector Dynamics as depicted here. We will show this in the next graphics.

Develop Exponential Power

Graphic 4:

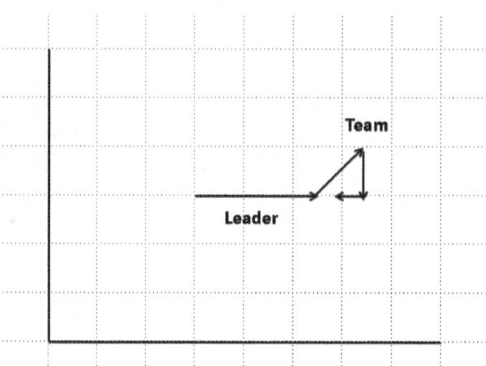

In Graphic 4 we have now added the Vectors together by adding them end to end. By doing this we will now get a clearer puicture on how strongly this team will pull toward the leader's goal. When we connect the beginning point to the very end we now have the actual level of push toward the leader's goal as depicted in Graphic 5.

Develop Exponential Power

Graphic 5:

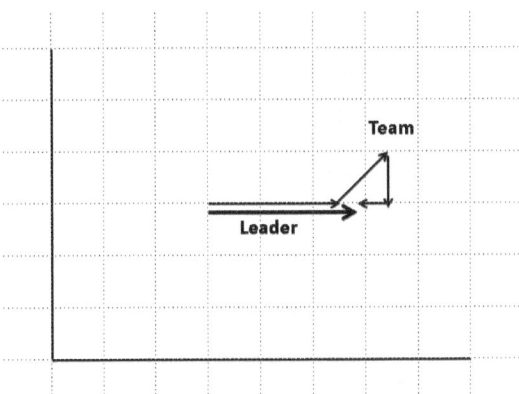

In Graphic 5 the summary and total push toward the leader's goal is represented by the thicker arrow. This is the sum total of the efforts of all team members combined, including the leader. I have moved the arrow slightly lower to improve visibility. Out of graphic 5 you see that even though our leader has three members on his team the combined push in this scenario is only a little bit greater than that of the leader herself.

The next question you will likely ask now is: What is the potential of this specific team if it were aligned in the same direction? Please proceed to Graphic 6 which should help in understanding this.

Develop Exponential Power

Graphic 6:

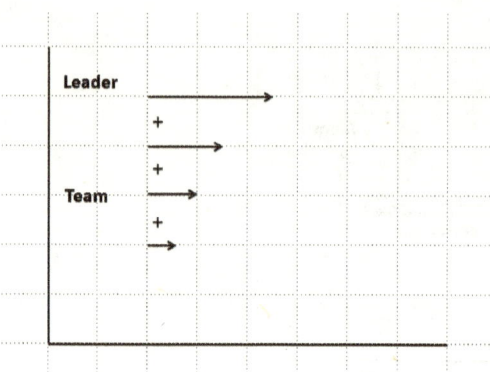

Here we have the invidual vectors shown separately yet aligned with the leader. What happens when we add them up?

Develop Exponential Power

Graphic 7:

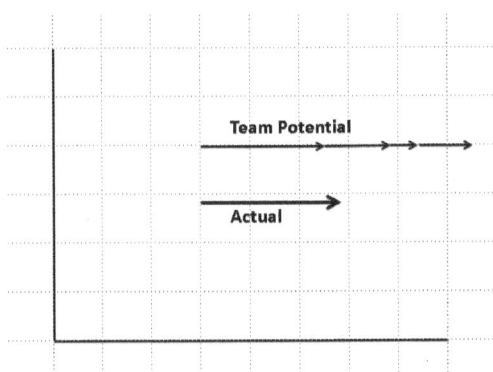

The upper, combined arrows depict what the team potential could look like after full alignment. This does not yet include any increase in motivation due to the alignment. Truly aligned teams are a force to be reckoned with. This particular team, through *alignment*, has now approximately doubled its push, energy, power or momentum in the direction of the leader's goal. Another way of looking at it is that it has gained by 100%, while before it had misappropriated much of its momentum.

This can be quite an eye opening experience for those of us who are leading teams, groups, or entire organizations. (Actual results will vary depending on actual team composition and alignment!)

The principle of *vector dynamics* and *alignment* also applies to individuals, by the way. Even within ourselves, we'll find that we're not completely in alignment with certain goals or targets we have. (Not surprisingly, these are the areas where we experience a lot of struggle or stress in our efforts to succeed.)

Once upon a long, long time ago I was up for a job at a higher level. Part of me wanted to get that higher level job because it meant some more money; another part of me *didn't* want that job promotion because it also meant a lot more responsibility.

When there are internal conflicts like these, it's literally like having two rowers in the same boat going in completely opposite directions! And that's why even on the level of our individual selves, it's important that we find alignment.

Any opposing values, beliefs or attitudes will fight against us and ultimately slow us down or keep us from achieving our goals.

EXERCISE

Find one area in your life where you've experienced a lot of struggle or conflict. It could be your job or a project, it could be one of your relationships, or it could be anything else. Examine that area and identify what elements, desires, or values are in conflict.

For example, maybe spending time on Facebook makes you happy, but it also distracts you from your work. Once you've identified the conflicting elements, see how you can create alignment. One option is to create priorities (e.g., work first, Facebook second); another

Develop Exponential Power

option is to create boundaries (e.g., focus on Facebook only after work hours); yet another option is to eliminate a conflicting element entirely (e.g., delete your Facebook account). Or yet another option is to find a way to use Facebook in a way that supports your work.

Now, creating alignment isn't easy and it can involve making tough choices. But living without it is even harder. In the absence of alignment, energy is just wasted—and that leaves you with a lot less power to fulfill on what you really want.

> *"We are what we repeatedly do. Excellence, therefore, is not an act but a habit."*
>
> ARISTOTLE

Develop Exponential Power

Develop Exponential Power

The Power of AUTHENTICITY

"The great majority of us ... live a life of constant duplicity. Your health is bound to be affected if, day after day, you say the opposite of what you feel, if you grovel before what you dislike, and rejoice at what brings you nothing but misfortune."

- BORIS PASTERNAK

In the chapter on TRUST, I talk about how trust depends on the affinity and affection between people as well as the level and quality of the communication between them.

Now, one of the biggest blocks that gets in the way of people's affinity for each other and communication between each other is the absence, or lack of, authenticity.

Do you think it might be more difficult to have people follow when the perception is that their leader is plastic, fake, or for some reason not quite truthful.

Develop Exponential Power

Leaders that are not authentic can be seen as low quality, cheap, untrustworthy, uninspiring, unworthy, unreal, worthless, less confident, even weak and scared.

Leaders that are authentic, however, are viewed as powerful, valuable, trustworthy, worthy of following, real, confident, inspiring, high quality, and having integrity.

There are many ways to define authenticity, but in this context, I'm going to define authenticity as our ability to freely express and communicate our experience.

Let me say that again in a slightly different way: Authenticity is our ability to say and share with others what we truly think and feel. Authenticity is to communicate what is truly so for us. Authenticity means it's real.

For the ladies among the readers, what would feel better for you? To have the purse of your dreams, or a knock-off? Naturally, the real thing feels much better, we can be confident about its quality and origin and we don't have to hide its fakeness. We don't have to pretend because it's the real deal. For men, that fake Rolex or Breitling won't give you the same feeling and confidence as the real one. And the super compressed MP3 you downloaded for "free" won't be as exciting as the lossless version you paid for in earnest.

When it's not authentic, then it's not real. When it's not real we could pretend that it is, but it might still make you feel cheap, ashamed, or guilty. When we feel cheap, ashamed or guilty, we feel less confident,

Develop Exponential Power

and guilt has robbed us of our power. When we are pretending it's like we're hiding behind something and it will be like putting ourselves behind the bars of a prison. Do prisoners have power? Of course they don't and neither do you when you're not authentic. Inauthenticity is a power-sucking prison or it may feel like a mask we wear to cover our real selves. I invite you to ditch that mask and escape from that prison.

It will provide you a level of freedom that will give you access to power you will have rarely felt.

Some of you might be reading this and be thinking: Well, it's all good to be authentic, but we can't just go around being unpleasant or disappointing or hurtful to people, right?

On the one hand, that's a valid point to make. But on the other hand, many of us are inauthentic even when there's no risk that what we're saying is unpleasant or disappointing or hurtful. In fact, many of us are inauthentic simply because we want to look good, or we want to fit in, or we don't want to be inconvenienced, or because we feel we might damage the relationship.

So even if it's an outright lie, even if it contradicts what we truly think or how we truly feel, we'll say something just to be polite, just to get off the hook and just to maintain the status quo.

But my question is: How much power is there when you hide yourself like that? How much power do you experience and how strong do you feel when you misrepresent what you truly think and feel?

Develop Exponential Power

I'm willing to bet your answer would be: Not very much and not very strong. Because the fact is, when you're not authentic, it's like putting yourself in that prison. You lose your freedom to express yourself and to be yourself, and your environment ends up dictating who you're going to be and how you're going to behave.

It's as if you're in a prison with the key lost and forever unavailable. Does a person without freedom have power? Does a prisoner have power? Let me tell you there is no power behind bars. A prisoner is someone who has lost all choice, and with the loss of choice you have lost your power. We always have the choice to be authentic and remove the bars around us. Yet when you're hiding behind inauthenticity it's like you're putting yourself behind bars. You have effectively imprisoned yourself and given away your power. You have become too afraid to be real; yes, it is fear, not politeness and not culture, that makes people inauthentic and unreal.

In short, you lose a huge amount of power when you're not authentic.

Besides the loss of power you experience when you're being inauthentic, there's also the loss of affinity, communication, and trust between you and the other person.

Why?

People can sense it and feel it when you're not being honest with them, and when that's the case, how can you genuinely expect them to be honest with you or

Develop Exponential Power

even trust you? Whenever one party in a relationship starts being inauthentic, it's only a matter of time before the other party starts being inauthentic too. Before long, the relationship will begin to deteriorate then fall apart altogether. The relationship will go into a downward spiral and die.

On the other hand, it only takes one person being authentic for the other party to start being authentic too. Haven't you noticed that in your relationships, especially at the beginning of your friendships? Someone who was once just an acquaintance suddenly shares something very intimate about themselves, and the next thing you know, you're telling them some pretty intimate details about your life as well. That's when the relationship shifts from a mere acquaintance to a real friendship.

Sometimes, the initiative to share something more personal comes from you. Regardless of who takes the initiative, my point is that once someone in the relationship makes the effort to be authentic, it usually inspires and encourages the others to be authentic as well. And you will now find that within you and within that relationship, there's affinity, there's communication, there's trust, and there's a new level of power.

EXERCISE

Go back into your life and identify at least one relationship where there has been a loss or lack of affinity, communication, and trust coming from an absence of authenticity. It could be with your mother-in-law (whom you're always trying to please), or it could be with your boss (whom you're always trying to impress), or it could be with your spouse (whom you're always trying to reassure). The point is: find someone in your life with whom you haven't been completely honest. Maybe you didn't lie to them, but you didn't tell them everything either.

Now here's the exercise: tell this person that you haven't been authentic with them and tell them why you were afraid of being authentic with them. Say what you need to say without holding anything back (you might need to read the chapter on COURAGE before you do this!). Be fully authentic with this person, whoever he or she is—and then see what it provides: for you, for the other person, and for the relationship itself.

Just one note about this exercise: being authentic with someone doesn't mean hurting them or insulting them. There is a way of expressing what's genuinely there for you, if it's unpleasant, and you can do this without being hurtful or offensive—and that's by telling the other person that what you're sharing with them is *your* experience of a particular action rather than an assessment of who they *really* are.

For example, instead of saying "You're mean and you belittle me all the time," you can say "Every time you say I can't do something, I allow myself to feel hurt and I allow myself to feel incapable." By pointing to a specific action and its specific impact on you, the other person gets that it's not *who they are* that's being attacked, like there's something wrong with *them,* but that there are certain things they DO that aren't workable for you.

Develop Exponential Power

Doing this can be tricky at first since we're more used to accusing people in general rather than pinpointing specific actions, but it makes a HUGE difference in how receptive people will be to what you're communicating to them.

And, I assure you that however it turns out, just making the enormous effort required in being authentic will already increase your level of power.

In addition it is helpful to use "Future-Based Language."

Future-based language is expressing what you want to say in a way that shows the listener what you want to happen rather than complaining about what you don't want. So instead of saying that you hate being interrupted, you could mention that you'd love it if they would allow you to finish your thought before sharing their own thoughts. Of course this couldn't be said in a sarcastic tone but rather in a tone that shows trust and partnership and mutual appreciation. The most successful people, leaders, teams and organizations always deploy "Future Based Language."

> *"Authenticity is the alignment of head, mouth, heart, and feet - thinking, saying, feeling, and doing the same thing - consistently. This builds trust, and followers love leaders they can trust."*
>
> - LANCE SECRETAN

Develop Exponential Power

The Power of BELIEF

"Believe nothing, no matter where you read it or who said it, not even if I have said it, unless it agrees with your own reason and your own common sense."

THE BUDDHA

People often think that the only basis for a belief is how true something is in reality. That is, we should only believe in things whose truth we can demonstrate (hence the saying "to see is to believe").

What people don't realize is that belief isn't just something that results from something being true. In fact, in many cases, it's our belief that *causes* something to be true.

Said another way, our beliefs don't necessarily need to depend on reality, because the power of our belief can actually shape and produce reality. Many of the things we now take for granted as real—like the possibility of flight or the possibility of space travel—became real only because of the power of belief.

This is really important to get because by not understanding this, people overlook or underestimate belief as a tool they can use to shape their lives. Worse, they end up unconsciously using their beliefs in ways that even set them back!

The most classic example of an unproductive or even damaging belief is the belief that we're not good enough. A belief like this prevents people from exploring and expanding into new opportunities, and when people don't explore and expand they can't learn, and when they can't learn, they certainly can't get really good at something. Hence, this is a reality-producing belief rather than a reality-dependent belief. (This goes for most of the beliefs we have of ourselves and of other people, by the way!)

An example of this from my own life is a belief I used to have that I couldn't speak in front of groups of people. I had lots of evidence for this belief, including the fact that I would stutter whenever I was talking to more than one person. So, because I believed that I couldn't talk to big groups (or even just small groups for that matter), I never attempted it. Because I never gave it a shot, I never got speaking opportunities—which only further reinforced my belief that I couldn't talk in front of groups of people. You get the picture.

I finally got to address my belief when I pinpointed its origin. My belief that I couldn't talk to groups of people started when I was in sixth grade. During a class exercise where we were asked to list down topics that we wanted to learn about, I wrote down that I wanted to study the battle strategies of Julius Caesar. When my classmates heard about what I wrote, they started laughing! And in that moment, I decided that the things that interested ME didn't interest other people and that they therefore didn't want to listen to anything I had to say. My fear of talking to groups of people therefore came from my childhood belief that people didn't want to listen to anything I had to say!

When I realized this, I got clear that my inability to speak in front of people was the result of a childhood belief that wasn't even based on anything accurate. Because my classmates laughed when they found out that I wanted to study Julius Caesar, I took their laughter to mean that: (1) they weren't interested in what I was interested in; (2) no one else could possibly be interested in what I was interested in; and (3) no one could possibly want to listen to me. But the facts are: (1) my classmates could have laughed for *other* reasons besides being disinterested; (2) many people *are* interested in Julius Caesar (or how else could the History Channel be so popular?); and (3) even if other people don't share my interest in Julius Caesar, it doesn't mean that they wouldn't be interested in listening to me.

When I finally let go of my childhood belief, the alteration in my ability to speak in front of people was just *amazing*. Now, I speak regularly to groups of 400 to 500 people. I don't stutter anymore, I enjoy myself immensely and my audience gets enormous value from what I have to say. That's a real-life example of how belief is shaping reality.

Look at it this way: whatever you believe about yourself, you're right. If you believe you can make it, you're right. If you believe you can't make it, you're also right. If the Wright brothers had believed that flight was impossible for human beings, they would never have invented the world's first successful airplane and they would have ended up being right.

So my question to you is: Which of your beliefs about yourself will serve you better? Is it the belief that you can't do something or the belief that you can do something?

I'm willing to bet on what your answer will be.

EXERCISE

Choose one thing in your life that you've always said you couldn't do. It can be a simple thing like dancing or a complicated thing like flying an airplane. Whatever it is, just do it.

In some cases, you'll need to take lessons. But whatever you end up doing, I only have one instruction: you really have to let go of your belief that you can't do it.

This is absolutely important, because if you don't let go of that belief, all your efforts will be doomed. You'll ignore or downplay your accomplishments and you'll exaggerate your failings and mistakes. At some point,

Develop Exponential Power

you'll give up altogether—and it's the giving up that will make your belief that you can't do it true.

So keep believing that you can do it and keep going for it. I promise you, you'll be surprised at what you can actually accomplish once you let go of all of your beliefs to the contrary.

For further ideas on how to change a belief please see the chapter I call The Power of INTERPRETATION.

"Keep your dreams alive. Understand to achieve anything requires faith and belief in yourself, vision, hard work, determination, and dedication. Remember all things are possible for those who believe."

- GAIL DEVERS

"Be patient, your blessings and dreams are coming into your life! Just keep believing!

- CASSANDRA MANUEL FANSIER

Develop Exponential Power

Develop Exponential Power

The Power of

CHOICE

*"You always do what you want to do.
This is true with every act.
You may say that you had to do something,
or that you were forced to, but actually,
whatever you do, you do by choice.
Only you have the power to choose for yourself."*

W. CLEMENT STONE

People often believe that the exercise of choice is limited to areas where the options or possibilities are tangible or concrete, and that when there's only one such option or possibility available, then they don't have a choice.

For example, people think that if the only way for them to pay a debt is to take on a job that they dislike, they will often say afterwards that they took the job because they "didn't have a choice."

But choice is a capacity that operates on many different levels—and the level of the tangible or concrete choice is

Develop Exponential Power

just one of the lowest. The Austrian psychiatrist Viktor Frankl, one of the few survivors of the Nazi concentration camps and the inventor of logotherapy, once said: "Everything can be taken from a man but one thing; the last of the human freedoms—to choose one's attitude in any given set of circumstances, to choose one's own way."

This is absolutely critical because there are many instances in life where we find ourselves without choices at the tangible or concrete level. But the lack of choice on this level doesn't need to lead to a loss of power on our part. Until the very last moment, like Frankl said, we will always have the power of choice—even if it's a power that will be limited to our choice of attitude alone.

It might be easy to belittle the value of this, but our choice of attitude is enormously powerful. For Frankl, his steadfast belief in the value of life in the face of all the horrors that surrounded him during the Holocaust made all the difference in his ability to survive—and he observed that it was the same case with other survivors as well. Prisoners that gave in to their resignation, on the other hand, literally died.

It's not likely that we'll face circumstances similar to Frankl's, and we're very lucky in this regard, but it doesn't mean that we can't benefit from the wisdom he gained from his experiences.

In my life, I've experienced the power of choice in the area of my relationship with my wife. See, in the same way that you have a choice with regard to your attitude, as Frankl pointed out, you also have a choice with regard to the things on which you focus. (You might want to read the chapter on FOCUS after this, if you haven't read it already).

If you look at your own relationships, particularly the romantic ones, you'll notice that in the beginning, everything's just *perfect*: the other person never does anything wrong. Then as time goes on and the relationship matures, suddenly the other person starts doing all kinds of things—*undesirable* things—that they *never* used to do before.

But the fact is, the other person never changed. It's just that at the beginning of the relationship, our focus is on all the things that we find desirable about the other person. All the other undesirable things are already there—we just never pay them any attention! But as the relationship progresses, our focus slowly expands to include everything that the other person does. So it's not that they suddenly start doing things that we don't like, rather, it's that we start noticing these things *for the first time*.

And this is where choice enters the picture, because what we focus on is also a matter of choice. When our relationships begin to sour, in many cases it's because we've begun to focus only on the things that we find undesirable. Just choosing to adjust our focus can have a huge impact on the quality of our relationships.

Choosing what to focus on was precisely what altered my relationship with my wife. When I chose to focus once again on what was great about her and what was

Develop Exponential Power

great about our relationship, I went from wanting to complain all the time to being grateful—in just a few seconds! The shift was just amazing.

The point is: choice gives us power, and because, as Frankl insists, we will always have a level of choice, then the good news is that we will always have a level of power.

EXERCISE

Find an area of your life that's disempowered you because you've always felt that you "didn't have a choice" in that area. Then ask yourself: what has your sense of disempowerment, bitterness, disappointment, frustration, and resentment in that area actually provided for you? Has it made a positive difference? Or did it just make things much harder for you?

If you find that your attitude or focus in this area has only made things worse, consider that your attitude or focus is actually a choice—and that you have a very real power to choose something else more empowering. (For pointers on how to generate a more empowering attitude, you can refer to the chapters on INSPIRATION and INTERPRETATION.)

Develop Exponential Power

"It is our choices that show what we truly are, far more than our abilities."

J. K. ROWLING

Develop Exponential Power

Develop Exponential Power

The Power of COMMITMENT

"Unless commitment is made, there are only promises and hopes; but no plans."

PETER DRUCKER

Commitment is an overly used word—and one that's often misunderstood. One of the ways people misunderstand commitment is by associating it with the word "try." People believe that to be committed means to try very hard in the area of one's commitment.

On the contrary, there's nothing more non-committal than the very notion of trying. One way I demonstrate this in my capacity as an executive coach is to have my clients do the following exercise:

First, I'll put a pen in front of my client. Then I'll tell him or her that I'm going to ask them to do two very different things. The first thing I'll ask them to do is to

Develop Exponential Power

"pick up the pen"—which they'll usually do without any difficulty.

Then I'll ask them to "*try* to pick up the pen"—and this is where things get complicated.

Most of my clients will go right ahead and pick up the pen. Then I'll shake my head and remind them that I told them at the start that they were to do two *different* things, the first of which was to "pick up the pen" and the second of which was to "*try* to pick up the pen."

At this point, most of them will think for a few seconds, and then go right ahead and pick up the pen. Then I'll remind them once again that that's *not* what I asked them to do. By this time, a few will look perplexed while a lot will look downright annoyed. Then for every instance afterwards that they'll pick up the pen, I'll just tell them all over again that the instruction was to "*try* to pick up the pen."

Some of my clients get this really fast while others take several attempts. Done correctly, "trying" will look something like this: my client will have his or her hand hovering in the air, but will never actually touch the pen. Or, they'll be touching the pen, but they'll never actually pick it up.

You get the picture.

If you try this exercise yourself, you'll notice that when you're "trying" to pick up the pen, it feels as if one set of muscles is pulling in one direction and another set of muscles is pulling in the opposite direction. It requires

Develop Exponential Power

twice the effort to "try" to do something and it also wastes a lot of time.

This is what I mean when I say that trying is actually very non-committal. Real commitment is just going right ahead and doing something.

Most people actually get this. For instance, have you noticed that when someone asks you to do something you don't want to do, and you don't want to say no outright, you often tell them that you're going to "try"? It's one strategy we've learned in order to be politely non-committal. In general, when we use the word "try," we use it in relation to areas where we're not very sure we'll actually succeed.

Children, on the other hand, *don't* try (they haven't learned the strategy yet). They go right ahead and do things. When they fail, they learn from the experience and go at it again. If you've ever watched a toddler learning to walk, you'll know what I mean.

EXERCISE

When you catch yourself saying "I'll try" in an area that matters to you, stop yourself and make a commitment instead. You can do this by simply saying when you'll get the task done.

Declaring a deadline is enormously effective because otherwise, you'll just put off doing your commitment to

Develop Exponential Power

"someday" (and if you've noticed, "someday" never appears on any calendar!). Stating a place is helpful too.

In my observation, commitments turn into reality much faster whenever a date and a place are attached to their fulfillment. Giving a commitment without stating when and where you'll get it done is like inviting someone to a party without telling them what time it'll start and where it'll be held.

So when a client asks me if I can send a proposal as soon as possible, instead of saying "I'll try" I'll say: "You'll have it on your desk by ten o'clock tomorrow." Or if I am busy that day I will ask them by what day they'd like to have it on their desk. By saying this to my client I have now effectively engaged them as an observer who will clearly be able to tell whether I am keeping my word, or not. By doing so I make sure I keep my commitment and also remain in integrity with my word.

Committing myself in this way has me do everything I can to fulfill the commitment—which vastly increases my power in getting things done and for one reason or another isn't it easier to keep our commitments to others versus ourselves?

Want to create an even greater level of commitment for yourself? Just do this: Pretend your life depends on it, or the life of someone dear to you. It is amazing what we can accomplish when life depends on it.

Develop Exponential Power

"Act as if life depends on it."

- BJORN MARTINOFF

Develop Exponential Power

Develop Exponential Power

The Power of CONTRIBUTION

"Act as if what you do makes a difference. It does."

WILLIAM JAMES

One of the least intuitive ways of generating power for yourself lies in being a contribution to other people.

I'll say that again in another way: one of the most effective ways you'll ever discover of empowering yourself lies in empowering others. And nothing is more fulfilling and nothing else will open more flood gates to success. When you are contributing, when you're making a difference, it's as if you are on the side of good, the side of God.

Now, I'm not saying this coming from the logic that the good that you do will always find its way back to you in the way you expect it to. The good you do will bounce back to you eventually though rarely in the exact way you expect it. However, what you can expect is that it will and that it does.

This truth is what some call *Karma*.

That Karma even exists may be difficult to get or swallow. But it certainly can be observed and experienced.

Let me explain.

Whenever I coach an executive who's nervous before making a big presentation, I usually ask him or her a very simple question: "At this very moment, what are you focusing on?"

I usually get some of the following answers:

"I'm wondering about how I look."

"I'm worrying about how prepared I am."

"I'm thinking about what they'll think."

"I'm hoping that I'm not going to make a mistake."

"I'm wondering if my pants are zipped."

"I'm worrying that I'm sweating too much."

If you look at all the answers above, you'll realize that they have one thing in common—which is that in all cases, the person is focusing on *himself* or *herself*. Whenever a client of mine starts focusing inwards

Develop Exponential Power

rather than outwards, that's when their nervousness begins.

The same thing happens to me too. Whenever I focus on myself during a presentation—either worrying about my appearance or worrying about my performance—that's when I usually start getting nervous and uncertain. My voice will start trembling. I'll start having difficulties looking people in the eye. I'll start losing my connection to the audience. I'll start losing my train of thought.

Then when I finally notice what's going on with me, I'll stop and ask myself the question that my friend Anthony Robbins always likes to ask: "What are you focusing on, Bjorn?"

And when I am nervous or anxious the answer will always be the same: "I'm focusing on *myself*."

But when I start focusing on the people in front of me rather than on myself, there's an *immediate* and *palpable* shift in my level of power. When my concern shifts from *am I doing it right* to *what will make a difference for my audience*, the anxiety fades, the nervousness stops and the uncertainty disappears. From that point onwards, the only thing that's occupying me is how to make a difference for my audience—there's literally no room to be worrying about anything else, least of all myself.

Now this can be counterintuitive for a lot of people. It seems to make more sense for us to focus on ourselves if we want to increase our power. But paradoxically, it's when we focus on others with an intention to be a

Develop Exponential Power

contribution to them that we're actually at our most powerful.

That's why it's not a coincidence that the most powerful people in history and in the world are the people who've made the biggest difference in other people's lives. Think about Nelson Mandela, the Buddha, Christ, Gandhi, Martin Luther King, Jr., Mother Teresa, and Princess Diana. They were enormously powerful people—and their lives were focused completely on others.

Now let me talk about what I mentioned earlier: which is that the good that we do for others eventually finds its way back to us.

When I was younger, my life was really just about me. I didn't care about anyone or anything else. I did pretty okay—but I was never as successful as I wanted to be.

Then for various reasons which I won't recount here, I eventually shifted my focus to include the welfare of *other* people around me.

And when I did, I noticed the most surprising thing: my success started to *take off*. Business was easier, achievement came faster, and I felt more fulfilled, more grateful, and more joyful.

Being a contribution allowed me to increase my level of achievement, and at the same time, a higher level of achievement allowed me to make even bigger contributions to others and my charities. The more I gave, the more I grew, and the more I grew, the more I was able to give. I gave away advice, money, and time—and I got them all back tenfold and in various ways.

A person though can't genuinely be a contribution if all they're after is getting something back.

The moral law of the universe will have you reap whatever it is you've sown. If you give, you will eventually receive. It's that simple. Just don't expect to receive something from the same direction that you gave, because I've found that the universe doesn't necessarily work that way. Sometimes, you can find your contribution coming back to you in completely unexpected—but always welcome—ways.

Being a contribution requires a lot of faith and courage though. (You might want to read the chapters on COURAGE and FAITH if you haven't done so already.) There are times in our lives when it's just difficult to be generous!

For example, when I first started tithing, which is the practice of giving ten percent of one's income as a contribution to charities, it was incredibly *hard*. To give that much income away when I didn't always have enough food in the refrigerator was *tough*.

But something always came through, and since I began tithing, my income has actually tripled (and even *quadrupled*) at times. *That's* the power of contribution.

But, you may say, Bjorn, I really don't have any money.

Develop Exponential Power

Even if you're not in a position to give money, you can always be a contribution in other ways. Besides tithing, for instance, I also support a non-profit organization in the Philippines that tutors underprivileged and academically challenged children. I don't just provide financial assistance to the organization—I also provide coaching and mentoring to its founder.

The point is: there are *so many ways* that you can be a contribution—and all you need is yourself and some time, and nothing else.

EXERCISE

Next time you're about to do something in an area where you don't have much confidence, ask yourself: "What can I do at this moment that will make a difference for the other people involved?"

Once you come up with something, focus all your attention on it for the rest of the time—and then see what a difference that makes for you and your level of power and confidence.

Develop Exponential Power

"Change your focus, from making money to serving more people. Serving more people makes the money come in."

ROBERT KIYOSAKI

Develop Exponential Power

The Power of COURAGE

"Feel the Fear and do it anyways."

SUSAN JEFFERS

It doesn't take any courage to walk through your apartment door. But it's a different story when that same door is engulfed in flames.

People quite often think of courage as the absence of fear. But courage is not the absence of fear. Rather, courage is acting *in the presence of fear.*

Let me say that again: courage is not the absence of fear, but the ability to act in the presence of fear. Your ability to act *in spite* of your fear is what courage is.

Develop Exponential Power

Why people often misunderstand courage is because people often misunderstand fear. In our culture, it's very easy to belittle fear. The popular view is that fear holds us back and gets in our way and it's therefore best to get rid of our fear (hence the slogan "No fear" that shows up on many bumper stickers and t-shirts).

But fear plays an important role in our lives by acting as a signal that we perceive a threat to our physical or psychological well-being. Without the presence of fear to warn us, we would likely act in ways that would jeopardize our safety, like tiptoeing on cliff edges, eating unfamiliar fruits, or manhandling snakes. So fear is useful and valuable and our lives would be harder and literally more dangerous without its presence.

What makes fear a little tricky is that it doesn't discriminate between different kinds of threats. You will have the same sensations and symptoms of fear facing a black widow spider *and* thinking of speaking in public (if that happens to be one of your fears). In the first instance, the fear is completely valid and it would be wise to walk away carefully and call an emergency hotline if you got bitten. In the second instance, the fear is completely counterproductive—especially when speaking in public will further your goals and intentions.

Unfortunately, most of the fears we have in our lives are like the second kind: completely counterproductive. This is why in the book, *The Teachings of Don Juan,* Don Juan tells the book's author, Carlos Castañeda, that fear is the first of our "four natural enemies" and therefore the first enemy we have to overcome.

Develop Exponential Power

This is where courage enters the picture. Courage is about taking action, not because fear is absent, but because we recognize that giving in to the particular fear we're feeling is counterproductive to our goals and intentions.

In my case, the desire to be courageous arose when I was very young. When I was just a little boy, I was scared of heights. My parents used to take me to the Stuttgart Television Tower, and by the time I was two meters away from the railing, I'd already be flat on the ground from terror. My father called me a coward for a long time because of this, and that triggered my desire to overcome fear.

Fortunately enough for me, I found good coaches and mentors later on in my life, and with their guidance, I started doing things that used to terrify me—starting with small and even silly things.

For instance, have you ever noticed that when people are riding an elevator, they are staring at the buttons like they're the most fascinating things in the world? No one says anything and no one looks at anyone else.

So one small exercise I took on was to *talk* to people in elevators—even if just for a few minutes. At first this was quite scary but at some point, I started having fun! The more courage I found, the more outrageous I got. I'd start telling people entering the elevator things like "Welcome aboard the Starship Enterprise!" Or: "Buckle up, you're in for the ride of your lives!"

Develop Exponential Power

And just this small exercise allowed me to overcome a big part of my fear of talking to strangers. The thing about overcoming a fear is that the first step is always the hardest—even if the first step doesn't look particularly scary.

But what's great is that every small step we take to overcome a fear slowly expands the range of our comfort zone. Once we've overcome one small fear, we've overcome it forever and we're ready to take the next small step. We keep pushing the edge of our comfort zone this way: taking one small step further, then another small step further, and so on and so forth, until, before we know it, our whole comfort zone has expanded beyond what we ever thought was possible.

What's also great about conquering fear is that overcoming a fear in one area of life seems to have an impact on our ability to overcome fears in *other* areas of life.

I usually put it this way: cultivating our courage is like blowing up a balloon—it's the *whole* thing that expands and not just one region. If we keep blowing up the balloon, it'll get bigger and bigger, until it becomes transparent and then one day it'll pop. When that day comes, you'll find that you really have no fear left anymore. That's when you'll know that you've practiced courage enough times to vanquish that first natural enemy.

You don't even have to start small. If courage is exercised whenever fear is present, then the greatest number of opportunities to practice courage can be found in the areas where there is the most amount of fear to face: namely, the areas of our dreams and aspirations.

It's in these areas where we go after what we want the most that we have the most fear, apprehension, and anxiety. That's why when people tell me that they have no fear, I'm left wondering if they truly have no fear, or, if they're simply not taking on anything challenging and are not going after what they really want. It's these areas that present the most valuable opportunities—and offer the greatest rewards—in cultivating courage.

EXERCISE

Commit to take on a small act of courage every day. I don't mean "do something stupid or reckless" or "put your life in danger." I mean taking action in areas where your fear is counterproductive—whether it's a small area or a big area.

So ask someone out. Say hello to a stranger in the elevator. Wear the shoes you always thought you'd never pull off wearing. Tell your mother and father you love them. Use every available opportunity to practice courage. By doing so, you cultivate it much faster as a habit, which will then allow you to use it for the really scary things in life (like finally asking someone to marry you or setting up your own business or buying your dream home even though the monthly payment is more than half of your monthly paycheck).

Develop Exponential Power

OPTIONAL EXERCISE

My friend Alan Feuerstein has a great way of dealing with fear. Whenever he's about to do something and he feels a little anxious or knows he's afraid, he treats his fear as if it was a person. He may even give him, or her, a name. I know it sounds crazy but don't knock it until you actually tried it.

Then he invites his fear to "Go sit on the chair, relax for a while, watch some television, and have some ice cream." Than in a very caring way he'll say to his fear: "Relax, I'll pick you up later when I'm done with what I need to do."

I find this lighthearted practice an effective way to deal with my own fear and I suggest that you try it as well. If nothing else, it's a great way to distract myself away from what scares me or makes me nervous. After that I experience myself getting into action much more quickly and powerfully.

So next time you feel a lump in your throat when you're about to do something you think is scary, just tell your fear, "I appreciate your inputs but I have to finish this email right now. Can you go sit in the corner for a while and relax and watch some television, please? And don't worry, I'll pick you up later when I'm done."

Develop Exponential Power

> *"Courage is resistance to fear, mastery of fear, not absence of fear."*
>
> \- MARK TWAIN

> *"It takes a lot of courage to release the familiar and seemingly secure, to embrace the new. But there is no real security in what is no longer meaningful. There is more security in the adventurous and exciting, for in movement there is life, and in change there is power."*
>
> \- ALAN COHEN

> *"Do the thing you fear the most and the death of fear is certain."*
>
> \- MARK TWAIN

Develop Exponential Power

Develop Exponential Power

The Power of DETACHMENT

"He who would be serene and pure needs but one thing, detachment."

MEISTER ECKHART

People typically think of detachment as the opposite of achievement, determination, or drive. That is, people tend to believe that if you're detached, you've given up on the idea of goals as a whole and that you've stopped going after them or even setting them altogether!

However, this is not what I mean by detachment. Here, I define detachment as the ability to let go of our emotions of attachment to the results of our efforts.

Let me repeat that: detachment is the ability to let go of our emotional attachment to the *results* of our efforts. It is *not* letting go of making an effort altogether.

Develop Exponential Power

Contrary to what many people think, detachment is actually crucial to achievement, determination, and drive.

Why?

Because if you're emotionally attached to a particular outcome, it is the fear of the emotion we will feel IF we fail that can stop us in our tracks before we even get started.

If you're emotionally attached to a specific way the outcome should look like, you're likely to get upset if that *EXACT* outcome isn't achieved. Getting upset will then only further block your progress by diverting your attention and energy away from the actions that could put you back on the path towards your goal. Emotional detachment is therefore essential in maintaining the focus and peace of mind that are necessary for accomplishment of any kind.

This can sound paradoxical to commitment and in some ways it is; yet try this on to see how it feels before you judge.

Detachment can even be extended to apply not just to the ends or goals we seek, but to the means that we employ in seeking those ends. Very often, we're attached to a particular way of accomplishing things—ways that have worked for us effectively in the past or we've seen work effectively for others.

Many times though, our preconceived notions of what's effective can often lead to the lack of results or even an

Develop Exponential Power

undesirable result altogether! Hence, detachment in this area means a willingness to let go of our attachment to how things *should* get done, or have always been done.

> *"We must be willing to let go of the life we have planned so as to have the life that is waiting for us."*
>
> - JOSEPH CAMPBELL

I learned this the hard way in my personal life—especially in the area of romantic relationships. For the longest time, I wanted to date a specific kind of girl, and my attachment to my criteria probably led me to miss going out with women who may have been a better match for me.

For instance, the first time I started dating after a long time of being single, I thought I might try to go out with an Italian girl. Sure enough, I met one within seven weeks, but my attachment to "dating an Italian girl" led me to overlook other things that were frankly more important in making a relationship last. So the Italian girl and I didn't last more than a couple of dates.

This type of relationship eventually became a pattern because I didn't understand what detachment meant. What I ended up doing again and again was to make my list of criteria *even longer*—which simply meant *expanding* the number of things to which I was attached.

Develop Exponential Power

After the Italian girl, for instance, I drew up a new list of attributes I wanted in an ideal mate that was a fully typed up *two* pages long. Again, the girl described on the list showed up in a few weeks, and again, the relationship didn't last. The relationship didn't last because on my two-page list, I'd somehow forgotten to include two very important requirements. One, being that she should be geographically within easy reach, and two, that she should also be *monogamous*. Well, the girl that showed up wasn't. So obviously the relationship didn't work out. I could have easily overcome the geographical challenge but the thing about her seeing more than one guy didn't sit quite well with me, if you know what I mean.

After that relationship ended, another two years went by and I finally decided to create *another* list, and this time I was going to make sure that I included everything I could possibly think of that was important. So when I was finished I had written up a list that was *eight* pages long.

I emailed it to my dear brother and highly respected friend Steve Miller in California to take a look. His immediate response: "You're crazy. *This person does NOT even exist!*"

Well I thought I have gone through all this effort. So I might as well see what happens.

And sure enough, a woman showed up in about eight weeks or so. She matched my list at least 96 to 98 percent, and even though we had a slow start we hit it off quite well and eventually got engaged. But again it wasn't more than a few months into the relationship that I realized that I had forgotten something that I should have included in my list. The item I forgot was that the parents should like me too. Du-uuh!

The relationship didn't last because once again, I'd forgotten to include something important on my list. Just so you know, they didn't even want to meet me because I wasn't a billionaire. I am talking US dollars here, AND I wasn't even famous. And since they were multi-billionaires, I obviously was a "salaryman" (it's what the Japanese call someone working for a salary) and I wasn't a fit for their daughter and never will be.

It took me nearly two years to figure out that it wasn't going to work. I wasn't even a millionaire, much less a billionaire which her parents wanted her to have. Nor was I a celebrity of any kind. So sadly, despite everything that was a match, the parents eventually won.

Again much time went by after that happened. I was confused, I didn't know whether I should be happy because the universe had fulfilled my order (the list) and given me what I wanted, or should I be upset because even though I had gotten what I wanted it didn't work out.

I was licking my wounds and needed healing. In addition everything else seemed to fall apart in my life. My finances went berserk and I lost my job. A theft at work left me depleted of my tools of the trade which the new owner of the company conveniently ignored. This was a huge monetary loss, but something inside me said it was good because it was time to move on and start a new chapter in my life.

It was in early 2003 when I did start a new chapter in life. I got rid of the cars, put everything else on eBay or in storage, and moved from Los Angeles to Asia and began to establish myself there. While the first couple of years in Asia were off to a good start, I had to go back to LA for a few months and earn some more money in order to either complete my transition or keep traveling through Asia. I was scheduled to be in Manila, Philippines in May to be working there on a Citibank project with some new friends. After completing the project, I wanted to spend some time traveling through India, and maybe spend time doing some more healing and learning at an ashram or two.

Life it turns out has surprises in store for you and sometimes when you least expect it. I had this feeling that something or someone special would come into my life on this trip but I had no idea as to when, or where.

It was great working with my friends on the first leg of the trip. On one weekend in Manila, someone suggested I attend this particular weekend seminar. I thought to myself, why not? Maybe I'll meet some interesting people. The seminar was starting on Friday morning. On Thursday evening I was at home in my hotel room near Manila's Ninoy Aquino International Airport. I was contemplating my life, the upcoming seminar, and the upcoming trip to India. I remembered how I had felt that something special was going to happen, an intuition if you will. I wondered if it was possibly going to happen while I was attending the seminar during the weekend.

Many times in my life I had spoken to my angels. Did you know that each of us has at least two angels? When I talk to my angels I always share with them what is happening in my life though I am sure they already know. Then I often ask questions for them to answer. Since I cannot "hear" their answers but rather get a feeling as an answer, I try to ask questions that can be answered with either yes or no. I always try to remember to thank them for their help.

Well I was talking to them that evening. Or maybe I was thinking about what to ask them as I was going through what had happened.

What happened was that on several occasions I had made a list of what I wanted in a woman and life partner. And each time, what I got nearly perfectly matched my list. And every time I got what I wanted on my list, it didn't work out. The relationship always went bust for one reason or another. Something was not quite right, I remember thinking to myself.

Eventually it came to me. I always seemed to forget that one thing to add to my list. And then I realized that I thought I knew best. I had believed that what was on my list is what's best for me. But was it really? I started to have a little doubt now. Reality had shown that it wasn't just important what was on the list, it was also very important what was NOT on the list or what was left out.

Develop Exponential Power

This time I decided to speak to God directly. And this is what I remember saying to him or praying to him. Dear God you have always given me what I wrote down and wanted. Every time you gave me what was on my list and I am grateful for that. However, in the process I have learned that I always seemed to forget to ask for that one additional thing. I always seemed to forget to ask for something. The list always seemed incomplete and I realized that I didn't know how to make a complete list for something as important as a life partner. For something much smaller, like a gadget or a car, it seemed simple enough, but in this case it seemed to have some additional complexities that I don't fully understand yet.

That was when I finally stopped and prayed to God and said:

"God, you know me perfectly. You have known me for a very long time, you know what I want and I think you also know what's best for me. I've been making these lists based on my own limited perspective, and none of them have worked because there's always something I end up forgetting or not realizing! So given that you have known me since my creation and know what I want and that you also know what's best for me, please give me that which is best for me in a life partner—possibly keeping my list in mind. Thank you."

And guess what happened next. The very next day, I was attending that seminar and I met Vicki—the woman who is now my wife and the mother of our four beautiful children.

Develop Exponential Power

Now, you don't have to be a believer for this principle to work. Whether you believe in a God or not and whether you pray to a God or not, what's critical is learning how to be detached, let God or the universe handle the rest. Have faith that the right thing is going to happen.

This is what I call Detachment. It is letting go of the emotional attachment to a specific outcome. Because when you want a specific outcome very badly, you might actually miss out on better opportunities that are staring you in the face or that are coming your way. Or when you're attached to doing something in a very specific way, you might miss opportunities for accomplishing your objectives in faster or more fulfilling ways. It's important to have intentions and it's important to be specific about your intentions—the key is in not getting emotionally attached to a specific outcome even when you're committed to it.

In the end, my wife Vicki "only" matched 75% of my list, but as of 2012, as I am putting the finishing touches on this book, we've been together for seven years and we now have four children.

Of course, detachment is much easier said than done. A few years ago, at a lecture I was attending in Los Angeles, a Buddhist master shared the following humble observation: "Detachment is easy when you're living in the mountains, when there's nothing tempting you or pressuring you. It's hard to be detached when you're living in the city and are surrounded by all the hustle and bustle." Since most of us don't have the luxury of living in the mountains, the only way we can learn detachment is through practice—and your practice begins with the following exercise.

EXERCISE

Next time you come up with a goal in a specific area of your life, carefully visualize what it would look and feel like in your life to have that goal fulfilled, to have it in existence NOW—and then let it go.

Keep doing this until there is no more emotional attachment and only commitment to the perfect outcome. In the process you might find the attachment coming back again and again. Don't worry because that's perfectly normal: just keep letting go. And when it comes back again, just let go again. It's a process. You know when you're ready when there is a sense of been there, and done that. Yet the commitment remains.

OPTIONAL EXERCISE

There's a particular practice I've found very effective in achieving a state of detachment, though it might not work for all people.

In stressful situations, I visualize a line running through the center of my head right between the centers of my ears. Then I imagine the exact spot on the line that's right in the middle between my ears. Now I focus on this center point until I get closer and closer and I feel that

that point is where I am—like it's the focal point of my entire being.

When I'm there solidly, it literally feels as if I'm sitting inside my head, piloting a robot, looking out from inside this robot that is my body, and with two windows that are my eyes. There's a marvelous sense of clarity and aloofness. I'm engaged and I'm in control, but there's none of the usual turbulence of emotion, reaction, or judgment. What is present is absolute detachment. It is something that the Buddha took a long time to achieve and you can get to in seconds. It works also well when stressed.

Now you can take this on as an exercise and then walk around and see what happens and how it feels. It might surprise you and feel a little uncomfortable at first because it is a place completely void of emotion and it may even feel a little scary as we're very much accustomed to feeling a constant stream of emotions.

Now if you don't find your center point automatically when you try this, just keep "adjusting" and probing in the surrounding area until you find where the spot is for you. Just keep trying until you get it—yet remember not to get attached!

Develop Exponential Power

"For all things and non-things that you may ever want, Friend, understand that sometimes the fastest way to get them is to forget them, and to focus instead on just being the most amazing human being you can be. At which point all of your heart's desires, spoken or unspoken, will be drawn to you more powerfully than a magnet is drawn to steel.

– MIKE DOOLEY

Develop Exponential Power

> *"When you keep yourself open to all types of possibilities & attach yourself to no one thing, that's when you will receive life's blessings."*
>
> *- MONICA BERG*

Develop Exponential Power

The Power of
EMPATHY

"When you start to develop your powers of empathy and imagination, the whole world opens up to you."

— SUSAN SARANDON

Likely the most important ability in life, business, leadership, marketing, sales, politics, and creativity is the ability to place yourself in someone else's shoes. Empathy is the ability to place yourself in someone's position and the ability to feel what they feel and understand the background of their thoughts as it relates to them. When this is achieved we have placed ourselves in a state of being called empathy.

Empathy creates a deep understanding for a fellow man or woman, your colleague, business partners, your customers, and even an opponent in warfare. Every husband wishes to understand his wife, every salesperson wishes to understand her clients, every general wishes to understand his enemy, and every player on a sports team wishes to understand the opponent. Empathy is when we can experience reality as they experience reality. It is what some refer to as the ability to place yourself in someone's shoes. When I can see someone else's reality from their perspective, I can gain a much, much deeper understanding of what it is they are going through, their experience of life, what it is they are feeling, what they might be thinking, and the reasoning going through their minds. I say "might" as there are different levels of empathy and the greater the level of empathy the more accurately you will experience the person's reality for yourself. Once achieved, the state of empathy will also allow you to see why and how they make decisions, with great accuracy to predict what their next move will be. Personally I see empathy as one of the most important tools of understanding my clients and my world.

The ability to feel someone's feelings, to vibrate on the same level they do, to hear their thoughts as if they were your own, will allow you to feel the vibration like a tuning fork picking up the frequency of an identical tuning fork.

Potential benefits of Empathy:

- Being able to more fully understand another person, client, market, or potential opponent
- Being able to sense another person's needs
- Helping another unload their load by making them feel understood
- Potentially being able to diffuse a situation with this knowledge
- Being able to foresee or more accurately predict the options and potential next steps of another person
- Understanding a foe or opponent and predicting their moves

Develop Exponential Power

- Potentially re-position yourself as an ally, mentor, coach, or friend instead of being seen as an opponent
- Transform a relationship
- Being able to understand and read your client
- Being able to read your target market
- Being more creative in developing solutions for others
- Being able to predict the market and create better products for a new or future market

Let's explain empathy further with the help of a metaphor. While metaphors are never quite perfect, they can be a great way of putting something into perspective. When we see the feelings and thoughts of a person as a package they want to deliver, then we can see them as someone wanting to deliver that package. And we can also see them suffering under the weight of that package all the way up to the point where they feel you have gotten it, the point when you receive the package, meaning you have not just received the message but also fully understood their reality. This creates trust when they want you to understand them or when they don't mind that you understand them. This trust in turn opens the door to all kinds of new possibilities, including new levels of relatedness, sales, market-share, battle field advantages, you name it, and you can see it in the list above.

When I used to be a supervisor at Mercedes-Benz in Beverly Hills, California I had 70 people under me. It wasn't unusual for me to have to deal with some sort of conflict between a couple of colleagues. When this happened, I would usually pull them into my office and have each of them share their side of what happened while the other had to listen openly and not allowed to talk until I said so. Once each had their opportunity to

Develop Exponential Power

share what happened, I had the first guy share the *intention* of what he did, followed by the second guy. Again neither was allowed to speak while the other was talking. This usually created enough empathy for both parties such that you could actually see and perceive from their faces that they understood, that it was just a big misunderstanding and that they actually quite liked each other. Empathy in most cases had been established in a very short time. But just to finish it off for good we discussed how we could have handled it better so that next time it won't escalate to that point. Simple really, but it takes a commitment to do it right, plus an assumption that we are all good people at our core.

In an Italian case study published in the September 2012 issue of *Academic Medicine* served "as a follow up to a smaller study published in the same journal in March 2011 from Thomas Jefferson University investigating physician empathy and its impact on patient outcomes. That study included 891 diabetic patients and 29 physicians and concluded similar findings: patients of physicians with high empathy scores had better clinical outcomes than patients of other physicians with lower scores."

In the end, when you don't understand someone, they won't easily allow themselves to be influenced by you if at all, or only with great resistance. You may still be able to persuade them to buy your product or idea, but likely it will be at a much reduced price and much less convincingly so. With empathy it will likely require a lot less arm wrestling if not a more immediate buy-in.

It is easiest to have empathy with someone who is being authentic with us, hence the importance of *authenticity* as explained in another chapter, and of course also *trust*. Without trust there is no authenticity. You can see how each beingness discussed in separate chapters empowers another and how they support each another, thus making their impact exponential.

Exercise

The simplest way to create empathy with another person is to simply feel yourself what they feel. They will be able to tell what you are feeling by the sound of your voice and the expression of your face as well as your body language followed by a short statement of understanding such as: *"I understand"'* Or *"I can get your reality."* Or *"I know how you feel"'*

To experience empathy with another person in more difficult cases, physically put yourself into their exact body language and situation. Make sure your entire body matches all of theirs. This includes the angle of their heads, every slightest millimeter of movement in their face, how they sit or stand, where they are looking, how they are breathing, how they position their shoulders. Give yourself permission to feel the feelings that come up no matter what they may be. You may also experience thoughts coming up as well as pictures of places and surroundings. In the beginning you may have to do this with your own body, while when you get better at this you might be able to do and experience this in your mind. Initially, it can take a bit or quite a few physical adjustments before you get it right the first few times but don't let that discourage you. The more accurately you match their physiology the more accurately you will be with reading them and feeling what they feel. Advanced practitioners may even pick up some of their mental images at that moment, no matter how distant in the past.

Develop Exponential Power

Welcome to the world of empathy. Empathy is a powerful tool in a world that has little certainty except for the certainty you create yourself.

"If you want to take someone to a new place, it is best to meet them where they are and then go there together."

- BJORN MARTINOFF

Develop Exponential Power

The Power of

FAITH

"Faith is taking the first step even when you don't see the whole staircase."

MARTIN LUTHER KING, JR.

Faith is certainty beyond logic and the ability to trust that a desired outcome, or at least an outcome that has your best interests at heart, will be the result of your efforts. It means being able to continue to work toward your goal, without doubting or stopping yourself or your initiative, when the result you're seeking hasn't yet materialized when expected or how you expected it. It also means focusing on what's missing in your efforts rather than giving up all effort entirely.

Based on everything I've said so far in this chapter as well in the chapter on Detachment, you already get a sense that having faith can be a challenge—especially in the times we live in when there's so much pressure to produce immediate results and when there is so much we could be doing "instead." We're often told to "do what's practical," or to "cut our losses" or to focus our energies on what's going to get "faster results." There's little room for just allowing time for our efforts to bear their inevitable fruit.

I learned how to have faith from a trying experience in my own life. Years ago, I helped turn around a small automotive company in Los Angeles. We were able to turn around this small company and bring it from losing a quarter of a million dollars per month to being profitable. Near the end we were having the highest customer satisfaction ratings in the region.

In that moment, just when I thought I'd be rewarded for my efforts and put on a corporate pedestal, the company was finally sold and I promptly lost my job. It was at this point, when things were at their lowest for me, that I took one of the biggest leaps of faith in my life: I got rid of my two Mercedes Benzes, sold a lot of things on eBay, put the rest of it in storage—and flew to Asia.

Given that I'd just lost my job when I'd actually accomplished something great, starting over again in a place that was completely unknown to me was practically insane.

But the day after I arrived in Asia, a door opened to the fulltime career I really wanted: a career in coaching, developing, and training people.

Today, I'm settled in Asia, with a thriving and fulfilling Executive and Organization Development business, a lovely wife, and four beautiful children. And what made it all possible was sheer faith.

Now if you're thinking that faith is something that's only for the religious, I can reassure you that it's not. Faith transcends religion in the sense that non-believers often exercise some form of faith in their lives. In fact, if you look into your own life, you'll find that some of your biggest accomplishments often came from your wildest leaps of faith.

So when you take a leap, hold on to Faith.

EXERCISE

Find an area in your life where maybe you've nearly given up on something because it seemed as if all your efforts were going nowhere. Find just one area—preferably one that really matters to you, like a hobby or a passion—and *commit* to taking consistent action in that area *even if you don't think you're getting any results*. Give yourself a time frame that's appropriate for what you want to accomplish. My only advice is: make sure your timeframe is longer than what you're comfortable with.

Because chances are, you simply haven't given enough faith and time in the past for results to be produced from your actions. In a lot of cases, faith is about being able to wait out that seemingly unproductive time and using it to learn whatever lessons need to be learned.

Develop Exponential Power

Try it—I promise that you'll be surprised and delighted by what happens.

"You are either living your life from Faith or you are living it from Fear. Most people live in Fear."

- JOE VITALE

Develop Exponential Power

"Faith consists in believing when it is beyond the power of reason to believe."

- VOLTAIRE

Develop Exponential Power

Develop Exponential Power

The Power of FLEXIBILITY

"Insanity: Doing the same thing over and over again and expecting different results."

ALBERT EINSTEIN

Once upon a long, long time a neighborhood was beginning to flood.

In one house there was a man all by himself.

A bus comes and the driver asks him to get on the bus to leave the area. But the man says: "No, God is going to save me."

Then the water rises to a height of several feet, forcing the man onto the roof.

Develop Exponential Power

A boat comes by to pick him up. But the man says: "No, God is going to save me"

The waters keep rising.

The man now sits on top of the chimney.

A helicopter comes by. But the man says: "No, God is going to save me."

The water keeps on rising and the man drowns.

Now he's in front of God and he asks God what happened. He says: "God, I thought you were going to save me!?!"

To which God replies:" Who do you think sent you the bus, and the boat, and the helicopter?"

While I don't know the source of this story, and I don't know whether it is true, it always makes me smile.

People usually think of flexibility as a notion that's opposed to focus. Focus tends to be associated with single-minded determination—like how a horse with blinders behaves—while flexibility tends to be associated with a kind of laidback looseness. Both are generally acknowledged to be positive traits, but are considered paradoxical when put together.

However, flexibility has an important role to play, especially when we already have the focus provided by having a goal or an objective. This is because not all the paths to our goals or objectives will take the form of straight lines. In fact, most of the paths that lead us to where we want to go never take the form of straight lines!

Focus, which I treat in a different chapter, refers to our ability to keep our final destination in mind regardless of the circumstances. It's our ability to keep our mind on our goal in the face of the many distractions and temptations that life throws our way.

Flexibility, on the other hand, refers to our ability to accommodate alternative and unanticipated ways of achieving our goals.

For instance, if you've decided that your dream vacation is a week in Bali, focus is sticking to "going to Bali" even if your travel agent keeps telling you that there's a promotion going on for a week-long vacation in Phuket. Flexibility, on the other hand, is being willing to take on traveling via ferries and buses instead of by plane so you can actually afford that week-long Bali breather.

That's why it actually pays to occasionally explore things that might be a bit "off" sometimes. I'm not telling you to scatter your energies all of a sudden in a hundred different directions. I'm just saying that every so often, it will do you some good to be willing to consider off-beaten tracks to your ultimate destination. So the $50,000 contract someone's offering you isn't the $1,000,000 contract you're looking for—but who knows? Maybe that much smaller contract will be the stepping stone to a series of contracts that will lead you to your $1,000,000 target.

Develop Exponential Power

The point is we can only see so far ahead. Opportunities often come up in the guise of seemingly trivial things, like invitations to parties or offers of blind dates. Synchronicity is something that we usually just see in hindsight: people look back and they suddenly perceive a trail of meaningful events that, at the time they happened, seemed completely disconnected and insignificant.

In my own experience, being flexible led to one of the biggest breakthroughs of my life. In the chapter on faith, I talked about how I eventually came to Asia from the United States. Let me say a little bit more about that move here, this time in relation to flexibility.

See, before I made my big move to Asia, I'd already determined what my purpose in life is, which is "to be a trusted advisor to world leaders." At the time I created this statement, Asia was definitely not on the list of places I had for fulfilling this purpose. So when I was considering going to Asia, it was a major concern to me that it seemed to have no connection at all with the purpose I'd set for myself. At the same time, something about Asia excited me. It also frightened me, to be honest, but the excitement was definitely there and it was stronger than the anxiety.

So even though I wasn't sure where it would lead in terms of my purpose, I still went for it. And sure enough, on my second day in the Philippines, I met a man whom I eventually ended up working with—and that partnership eventually led to me being able to express my skills and passion to a professional career in training and development that allowed me to get closer and closer to fulfilling my life purpose!

Here's what else being flexible provided for me: when I first created my purpose of being "a trusted advisor to world leaders," what I had initially meant by that was *political* world leaders. The leaders I eventually ended up working with were *corporate* world leaders. If I'd been stuck on just working with political world leaders, I'd have ended up being dissatisfied and unfulfilled. But being flexible about the kinds of leaders I work with has allowed me to flourish in my career. I wouldn't say no to working with political world leaders, I am still very much inspired by that AND, I'm very happy to be working with corporate world leaders.

That's yet another benefit of being flexible, by the way. You give God, and the universe, the chance to give you something that might lead you to even greater happiness! And not only that as it may eventually lead to something even more fulfilling.

So in your life, be alert to these seemingly random opportunities. Whenever they come up, ask yourself: what's being presented to me at this moment? Because the path to your goal may not look like anything you'll ever expect! And likely it will still lead you in the direction you have wanted to go all along.

Develop Exponential Power

EXERCISE

Go back into your life and start paying attention to the different opportunities that come your way and see how they might be alternative ways of reaching a goal you have in mind.

For instance, you might have always wanted to develop or strengthen your leadership skills, and you've been waiting for your job promotion as a chance to do precisely that. Then a friend invites you to take a martial arts course, and you instantly dismiss it because "it's not your thing."

But if you ask me, for instance, I've learned some crucial aspects about leadership just from watching Bruce Lee—lessons that I now teach to my executive coaching clients and which they hugely appreciate. But that connection between leadership and martial arts won't necessarily be so obvious—and that's exactly why flexibility is necessary.

So when opportunity shows up, trust, be flexible, have faith, and go for it!

Develop Exponential Power

"In the future, instead of striving to be right at a high cost, it will be more appropriate to be flexible and plural at a lower cost. If you cannot accurately predict the future then you must flexibly be prepared to deal with various possible futures."

EDWARD DE BONO

Develop Exponential Power

Develop Exponential Power

The Power of FOCUS

"One reason so few of us achieve what we truly want is that we never direct our focus; we never concentrate our power. Most people dabble their way through life, never deciding to master anything in particular."

TONY ROBBINS

In the everyday understanding of the word, focus refers to the point on which we train our attention and concentration. Most people are already aware of the importance of focus, but what most people don't know is that there's such a thing as primary focus and secondary focus.

Primary focus and secondary focus are concepts I learned from a race car driving instructor back in the

Develop Exponential Power

days when I worked for Mercedes-Benz in Beverly Hills, California. According to him, it's crucial in race car driving to look ahead to the farthest point of the track that you can still see. This farthest point of vision is what is known as primary focus, and the intention behind training your attention on it is to avoid surprises such as rocks on the road, potholes, or other surprises that can get really nasty if you see them too late.

I learned this the hard way when I was about 24 years old. On a dark night, I was exiting a small village on a German highway. I was driving with a couple of friends in my freshly restored 1967 Buick Skylark convertible. With the Buick's 5.7 liter V8 engine, it occurred to me that I could easily overtake the five cars ahead of me all at once. Not having any idea of what the primary focus was at the time, all my attention was on the first car I was attempting to overtake. Just when I was driving past it, the third car up ahead pulled out of its lane and got onto *my* lane to overtake the car ahead of it—and I was right behind this car *at 200 kilometers per hour and accelerating.*

Through an unimaginable stroke of luck, I was able to avoid the car. I hit the brakes HARD, the car swung around hard with the rear brakes locking up and we ended up on the other side of a big ditch and in the middle of a muddy corn field. Luckily I didn't hit the other car and nobody got hurt, but there was a LOT of damage to my Buick. The front end, the grill, and the hood were badly warped.

Develop Exponential Power

Looking back, if I had kept *all* the cars ahead in my field of vision by focusing on the furthest car ahead and not just on the one that I was trying to overtake, I likely would have been able to make the necessary corrections quicker and sooner and avoid the entire mess in which I had suddenly found myself.

And this is a mistake novice car drivers tend to make. Most new car drivers will only focus as far as fifty to one hundred meters ahead. Such a limited field of vision prevents us from seeing obstacles further up ahead such as rocks, potholes, and even a small child running across the street. By the time we notice them, we'll only have a few seconds left to react—not enough time in a lot of cases to choose the appropriate response, much less the desired outcome or result.

As it happens in driving, it also happens in decision-making. Often, we make the wrong decisions because so little time is available to thoroughly consider them. These wrong decisions then delay us from achieving our goal by either getting us off track, or worse, derailing us altogether.

> *"He whose gaze is fixed on a distant star will not falter..."*
>
> \- LEONARDO DA VINCI

Develop Exponential Power

So in life, just like on the road or on the race track, it's important not just to focus on the immediate objective you have in mind—the secondary focus—but on the ultimate objective that lies far ahead in the horizon—the primary focus. Secondary focus means looking ahead to where you immediately need to go while primary focus means looking ahead as far as possible. The beauty of focusing way ahead is that what is near stays in your field of vision even when you focus way ahead.

EXERCISE

Take a long-term goal you have in one area of your life and break it down into intermediate objectives or milestones. Milestones are smaller-scale achievements that function as stepping stones to your ultimate goal.

For example, if your long-term goal is to run a marathon, good milestones would be quitting smoking, buying running shoes and finishing a 10-kilometer run. Milestones are good ways of assessing whether you're on track to achieving your goal or not. In the context of focus, your end goal is your primary focus and your milestones are your secondary focus.

So while it's good to devote your attention to getting your lungs in shape and in getting the right kinds of footgear, every so often it's worthwhile to just "look up" and out into the horizon and to remember what it's all for—which is to run or even win a marathon.

Develop Exponential Power

Focusing way ahead will keep your decision-making in alignment with that primary goal. It will help guide you to make the right choices and decisions along the way. But if you only focus on the next step, the choice you'll make may be appropriate for that next step but may not necessarily be the appropriate choice for your long-term or primary goal.

Note: Hence, in a corporate setting it is very useful to open meetings revisiting that vision, your corporate purpose and values as well as your long-term goals briefly to get everyone into the right frame of mind.

"Concentrate all your thoughts upon the work at hand. The sun's rays do not burn until brought to a focus."

- ALEXANDER GRAHAM BELL

Develop Exponential Power

Develop Exponential Power

The Power of FUN

> *"People rarely succeed unless they have fun in what they are doing."*
>
> DALE CARNEGIE

The subject of power can be invested with so much significance that it's rarely, if ever, associated with having fun. But if we stop to consider it, we're most compelling when we're having fun, most productive when we're having fun, and most effective when we're having fun. Hence power is a by-product of having fun and I've seen this demonstrated by what my friend Jim has achieved.

Jim used to run a car dealer—one of the best in California and in the world. He transformed it from a tiny dealer in an out-of-the-way suburb into one of the

Develop Exponential Power

biggest dealers in Los Angeles in just a few short years. At the time that I met him, he had just succeeded in growing his business 20 percent the previous year in a market that had actually shrunk by 20 percent. How Jim did it was by having fun—by transforming what his people would otherwise think of as mere work into challenging and enjoyable games. On the floor, I've seen him invent spontaneous games, once yelling at the top of his lungs that "the one who sells the next car gets an extra $2,000!" He would do this sort of thing regularly though it would have lots of variations. I do hope he will write a book about his experiences in the near future.

Jim actively applies what many of us have always instinctively known: that having fun is important and that relating to what we do as a game is empowering.

We not only perform better when we're having fun and when things are going well, but the fun also offsets the less pleasurable emotions that inevitably come up in anything that we do—especially during periods of crisis or setback. Fun makes it easier for us to persist even when we're not succeeding because we are genuinely enjoying the process rather than being merely attached to its outcome. And one of the best ways for us to have fun is to re-contextualize or reframe what we're doing into a game.

So if you want to have power in a particular situation, see if you can turn what you're up to into some kind of game, where playing the game, and eventually winning can be fun for you and those playing the game with you. Just be responsible and make sure that what's fun for

Develop Exponential Power

you doesn't harm someone else! Ideally everyone else will have fun as well.

EXERCISE

Look at your goals and see what kind of games you can create around them that will make them fun for you to win. For example, one game I frequently play is the game of treating-myself-to-a-full-body-massage-if-I-win-a-client-tomorrow or a dinner with my wife at my favorite place for finishing a proposal on time. Of course, it's easier to create fun games in some situations than others, such as paying off a debt or making an apology. But the more challenging the circumstances are, the greater are the likely rewards.

One last thought: whenever possible, include your family, your friends, your colleagues, and, when possible, even your clients in the games that you play.

Fun is infectious, and the more people have it, the more it will empower you, as well as those around you, to succeed.

Develop Exponential Power

The Power of GRATITUDE

"Gratitude makes sense of our past, brings peace for today, and creates a vision for tomorrow."

- MELODY BEATTIE

One of the simplest and most effective yet also most overlooked ways of generating the inner power that propels us forward lies in choosing to be grateful.

In the chapter on INTERPRETATION, I talk about how power can be generated by choosing particular ways of interpreting life or viewing life. Gratitude is one of those ways of looking at life that's enormously empowering.

Why? Because in choosing to be grateful, you start focusing on all the things about yourself and your life that deserve to be appreciated. This in itself is already an enormous benefit given that we almost never think about what works in our life. (We're usually too fixated on all the things that *don't* work in our lives!) Here is what gratitude achieves:

- ☐ We correct the usually distorted view we have of ourselves and our lives by being present to what's good rather than just the bad.

- ☐ We realize that life isn't so bad after all, or that things *aren't* even bad at all and that they are actually quite good.

- ☐ We start to realize that even that which we relate to as "bad" might have some purpose to serve or some lesson to teach.

- ☐ We start to realize that we possess far more resources or capabilities than we ever thought we possessed.

By simply introducing a more balanced perspective or by getting us present to the blessings in our life, gratitude makes us not only feel better. It gives us enormous power.

But gratitude also serves a very practical purpose—which is to preserve and even increase the presence of that for which we're grateful.

How?

Well, if you believe in the Law of Attraction, which is simply a statement of the principle that like attracts like, then gratitude simply attracts more gratitude. Said another way, the Law of Attraction states that we tend to bring about that which is the constant focus of our attention. Since gratitude allows us to focus our attention on what we enjoy and like having in life, we end up having and attracting even *more* of these things in our life.

Conversely, when we're not practicing gratitude, we're usually griping about what we *don't* like having in our life. Following the Law of Attraction, by keeping our attention on what we don't like, we end up having and attracting even *more* of what we don't like.

Even if you don't believe in the Law of Attraction, the argument that gratitude helps preserve and even increase the presence of what we're grateful for still holds.

Why?

Because when we appreciate something, we exert more effort to take care of it and not squander it. What we're not grateful for tends to disappear or deteriorate because of neglect.

When you start feeling grateful for your health, for instance, you'll find yourself doing more to stay healthy, like eating less, and exercising more. Or when you start feeling grateful for your children, you'll find yourself spending more time at home and less time in the office. And by taking better care of your health or spending more time with your children, you'll end up with *more* in these areas for which to be grateful.

Develop Exponential Power

How I personally practice being grateful is that every morning, I light a candle on my altar and I thank God for every single aspect in my life for which I'm grateful. I give thanks for my business, my clients, my wife and my children—especially my children. I do this every morning and it sets an amazing tone for the rest of my day.

Now here's the bonus about gratitude: it's really easy to apply and a lot of its benefits are instantaneous. Some of the exercises in this book aren't necessarily fun to do because they ask you to confront certain things, but being grateful is one of those fun exercises that also provide instant gratification. Just try the next exercise and see for yourself.

EXERCISE

Look into your life and identify the areas where you're unhappy, upset, discontent, or resigned. The area can be your career, your family, your health, your spirituality, or even all of the above.

Write down all of these areas, and then one by one, start listing all the things in these areas for which you can be grateful. It can be something small (e.g., not having a car means I get to walk and exercise; not having a job yet means I get to spend more time with the children; etc.). It can even be something that hasn't even happened yet (e.g., I'll be a much stronger person after this setback; I'll finally learn how to be independent after this breakup is over; etc.).

Develop Exponential Power

The point is: Don't hold back. Get creative and even have fun! I promise you that doing this exercise will have an immediate impact on your level of being and power. And when you take on practicing gratitude on a regular basis, you'll be expanding your power even more, likely exponentially.

"As we express our gratitude, we must never forget that the highest appreciation is not to utter words, but to live by them."

- JOHN F. KENNEDY

Develop Exponential Power

Develop Exponential Power

The Power of

GROWTH

"All the evidence that we have indicates that it is reasonable to assume in practically every human being, and certainly in almost every newborn baby, that there is ... an impulse towards growth, or towards the actualization."

- ABRAHAM MASLOW

I once asked my friend Angie what she thought of whenever she heard the word "growth."

Her answer to me was: "Pain."

"Pain?" I asked. "What is it about growth that you find painful?"

She said: "Having to change everything all over again."

Develop Exponential Power

Angie's honest response expresses something that we all feel in different degrees about growth—that growth is uncomfortable because it involves *change.*

But why do we even dislike change to begin with?

Very simply: human beings dislike change because change disrupts our sense of certainty, predictability and control—the three things that contribute to making us feel *safe.* Knowing how things *are* allows us to anticipate how things *will* be—and by anticipating events, we can better keep them in check and control them.

For instance, knowing that a paycheck is going to come in regular two-week intervals allows us to plan and time our expenses in a particular way. But when the timing and frequency of that paycheck is suddenly changed, say to once every quarter instead, that alteration means having to adjust everything that's related to how we spend our money. That adjustment is often quite difficult, because it involves developing new habits of thought and new patterns for action.

I had a personal experience of this early in my career. For a few years, I worked part-time with a consultancy that was completely unpredictable when it came to paying their associates. Sometimes it took three days for me to get paid; sometimes it took a year. It was a very disconcerting time for me because I couldn't plan my financial future working with a company like that. I had no idea what was coming or when it was coming. In the end, I removed myself from that association even if it was a significant source of income because the money simply wasn't worth all the stress coming from the uncertainty.

This is why human beings can find growth painful. Growth is painful because growth *always* involves change—change that unsettles our sense of certainty, predictability and control. We're conditioned to believe that growth is a good thing, yet we find ourselves resisting it at times (maybe even a lot of times). Why we resist it is because we know it will involve change, and change means we need to do the work needed to adapt.

But what people need to realize is that even if growth and change are painful (or at least inconvenient), growth and change are also indicators of our vitality and power.

For instance, if you look at plants, a plant that isn't growing is literally a plant that's already dying. The same applies to human beings: as much as we need certainty and stability, we also need change and variety. My friend Anthony Robbins hit the nail on the head when he said that two of the six fundamental human needs are certainty and variety. The two might seem to contradict each other, but the fact is, being human often involves balancing paradoxical things.

So to go back to growth: when we don't grow—or when we refuse to grow—a little piece of us dies. We might get more and more comfortable keeping things exactly the way they are, but we'll discover over time that the comfort and the convenience don't really make us happy. In fact, they might lead to us getting downright depressed. And that's simply because as human beings we're designed to grow—and when we're growing and

Develop Exponential Power

expanding, we're becoming more of who we are and who we are is powerful.

EXERCISE:

Take a class. Do a course. Read a book. Learn a language. Meet someone new. Whatever it is, grow and develop yourself in at least one area. It might be uncomfortable and it might be inconvenient, but I promise you that it will expand your level of power.

"I have never let my schooling interfere with my education."

MARK TWAIN

Develop Exponential Power

"Intellectual growth should commence at birth and cease only at death."

ALBERT EINSTEIN

Develop Exponential Power

Develop Exponential Power

The Power of HUMILITY

"The most positively impactful and memorable leaders in history have always been both powerful and humble."

BJORN MARTINOFF

Humility is something you might not expect in a list of chapters in a book about power. How, you may ask, is humility related to all the other chapters that are greatly empowering to me?

Let me step back for a moment and ask you whom do you see as the most powerful people in history. I mean those who had a positive impact. Not those that had a negative impact on history.

The kind of people that come to my mind are Nelson Mandela, Martin Luther King, Mother Teresa, Jesus

Develop Exponential Power

Christ, The Dalai Lama, Mahatma Gandhi. All of them are unquestionably powerful people, having influenced millions of lives, even nations and entire generations.

What made these people so successful? What made them so impactful? Why did people listen to them? Why are they still remembered, even today, as some have died long ago? Yes they were exceptional, as they all achieved amazing results, and yes they did extraordinary things that nobody had done before, and yes they were some of the most influential people on earth. Yet they all had one quality that distinguishes them from other powerful people, and that quality or characteristic is HUMILITY.

The most powerful people in history were not just powerful, they were powerful AND humble. Now how can this be? Wouldn't Power and Humility contradict each other?

The answer is No. They actually support another. In a way like Yin and Yang balance each other out and make each other even more effective. Humility without Power won't get you anywhere. And Power without Humility will likely become FORCE. And we all know that people, when pushed or forced, tend to push back and resist. It is Humility that opens doors, opens hearts, and opens minds. It gives people choice and the option to align. Humility provides the choice to buy in, while force will arm wrestle, maybe even sell but rarely inspire.

In another instance, for decades I have been observing the German Soccer Team during the World Cup. I am not a huge soccer fan but I almost always watch the World Cup. I don't just cheer for the German team alone even though I was born in Germany, but I find myself cheering for other teams as well. Mind you 10 years ago the Koreans were the great surprise and made it quite far during the soccer world cup. They have since been in my heart. Or one time it was an African team that just amazed me with its super quick and elegant players. They were really something.

But back to the German Team, there appears to be a pattern in how they perform during a world cup. What I have noticed is that when the German team does really well in the first round of elimination, they usually won't win the World Title. However, when they seem to struggle and barely make it through the first round, that is when they seem to do really well all the way to the end and there is a good chance to capture the World Title.

What I noticed is that when the team is too sure of itself, when they do well easily, they don't take their next games as seriously. And sure enough because of this, they tend to be taken by surprise by other teams. The consequence is that they lose their games and the chance to become World Champions.

There is a real lesson to be found in Humility. When we're too sure of ourselves, we tend to take things too easy and because of that we tend to make mistakes.

Practice:

In practice when I notice I'm becoming too sure of myself, I remind myself to remain humble. There have been occasions in my life and career when I thought I

Develop Exponential Power

knew it all and guess what happened next? Life proved to me that I didn't! And it tends to be a pretty humiliating experience when this happens.

Now I just remind myself to remain humble in the first place. Will it be a piece of cake always? Not really. It's a practice to take on.

The more I practice the better I become.

"Don't be humble... you're not that great."

GOLDA MEIR

Develop Exponential Power

"Humility is a necessary veil to all other graces."

WILLIAM GURNALL

Develop Exponential Power

Develop Exponential Power

The Power of INSPIRATION

"You have to find something that makes your soul sing, something that's going to pull you forward naturally and effortlessly."

- BJORN MARTINOFF

People usually think of inspiration as something that happens mostly to artists and geniuses. If we happen to feel inspired every so often, that's a great thing. But feeling inspired *all* of the time or even *most* of the time seems like a lot to ask for and expect—especially for "normal folks" who aren't engaged in really "creative" work.

But I assert that the absence of inspiration from our daily lives is what turns our commitments into shackles. Commitments, duties, obligations, and responsibilities which are devoid of any inspiration become lead weights—things that, at the very least, hold us back from what we really want, and at the very worst, actually drag

Develop Exponential Power

us down and reduce that power available from within. Said another way, they become things that we *dread*:

Dread. Dread. Dread. Dread. Dread. Monday...

Dread. Dread. Dread. Dread. Dread. Wednesday...

Dread. Dread. Dread. Dread. Dread. Sunday...

Dread. Dread. Dread. Dread. Dread. A quarter later...

Dread. Dread. Dread. Dread. Dread. Five years later...

That which we dread and what we usually call a "job" or a "relationship"—and for those of us who've done the dreading long enough, we usually call it a "career" or a "marriage." Hence if our jobs or relationships don't last, many times it's because the inspiration has disappeared.

At this point, you might be asking: "But isn't inspiration beyond my control? Sometimes I feel it and sometimes I just don't! It's not like there's something I can actually do about it."

On the contrary, you *can* generate inspiration. If you look at all the things in your life that have inspired you—that have filled you with passion and incited you to take action—you'll notice that there's probably a pattern to them. The more you can identify what this pattern is and the clearer you are about what's common behind all these incidents, the greater will be your ability to generate inspiration for yourself.

Why?

Develop Exponential Power

Because the moment you know what inspires you, you can start looking at all your commitments, duties, obligations, and responsibilities from the perspective of your inspiration.

For instance, if alleviating poverty inspires you, and you're working (maybe not very happily) as a top executive in a multinational corporation, you can pause to consider how your work actually *helps* create jobs in the market and thereby alleviates poverty in a very significant way. Just like that, something that was a lead weight in one moment becomes a pair of wings in another moment. Imagine the kind of power you'll have in your work (and in your relationships) when you actually start seeing them as ways to fulfill what inspires you!

Now, when you start looking for what inspires you, here's a tip:

It's likely something that challenges you *enormously*.

I'm not making the above statement as a prescription—like it's something you *should* do. Rather, I'm saying it as a description—as something, in other words, that I've seen based on a lot of experience.

For instance, part of the work I do when I coach executives is to ask them to come up with ideas on how they can grow their business by 8 percent in one quarter. It usually takes a long time for the group to come up with suggestions, and they're usually not voiced with a lot of enthusiasm.

Develop Exponential Power

But when I ask the same group to think of how to grow their results by *200* percent, suddenly the entire room lights up! Everyone starts coming up with ideas and I have to struggle to write down everything they're saying fast enough.

So based on my observations, asking people to deliver 8 percent barely gets them going. Ask them to deliver 200 percent instead, and it's as if they've drunk 10 cups of coffee!

Why is this so? Logic tells us that it should be easier to develop ideas around an 8-percent goal versus a 200-percent goal. But that's never been the case in my experience. This is why I assert that human beings are *wired* to find inspiration in going after what *challenges* them.

You can see this by observing children or even just by remembering how you were as a child. When you were five years old, I don't think you said "I want to grow up and be second best!" or "I want to grow up and settle for something less than what I want!" No, I assert that when you were five years old, you probably said things like: "I want to be president of the country when I grow up!" or "I want to be an astronaut and walk on Mars!" or "I want to be a prima ballerina and dance in front of royalty!" or "I want to be a scientist and cure AIDS and cancer!"

In other words, we just *aren't* built to be inspired by small games. For instance, if you were given the choice, would you rather devote your life to inventing a tool that could save the lives of 500 people or one that could save the lives of 5,000,000 people?

I'm willing to bet on what your answer is likely to be.

For me personally, I've observed that it inspires me a lot more to talk to the top executives of an organization rather than its middle managers. This isn't because I have something against middle managers, but because my intention is always to make the biggest difference possible with the training programs that I offer. And when I'm talking to the head of a company rather than the head of a department, I'm clear that I have an opportunity to influence the lives of 2,000 people versus, say, 200 people. And that's something that personally inspires *me*.

EXERCISE

Take a look into your life and see if there is an existing area that you'd like to be more inspired by. Or see if there is an area you are still creating for which you would like to be more inspired. Pick the area or task that, if transformed, can give you the most juice in life. Ask yourself: *How can I re-contextualize, reframe or give some new, exciting meaning to this area or task so that I can't wait to get out of bed in the morning just to do it?*

Now, don't feel bad and don't give up if you can't come up with an answer right away. If this job, career, or relationship has been dreadful to you for years, it's perfectly understandable for you to find the exercise enormously challenging.

Develop Exponential Power

If you're in this situation, one way to start is by identifying all the aspects of this area or task that somehow contributes to your fulfillment. List down even the smaller ones that inspire you no matter how insignificant they may be. This might demand a lot of objectivity and generosity on your part, but stick to the exercise. Do it over several stretches if necessary, but don't stop until you begin to sense a glimmer of that inspiration that you haven't felt in a really long time.

Now, just a brief note: While there is such a thing as a right or wrong source of inspiration, people think that only the "lofty" goals in life are worthy of inspiration (like Truth or Justice or Peace). In general it can be more of a source of inspiration when many people benefit from the outcome versus just a single entity. What's also crucial is how *challenging* the source of your inspiration is, not because I want you to have a difficult life, but simply because if something doesn't challenge you, it's just not likely to inspire you!

So the true test in assessing a source of inspiration is in how it literally *gives you life*. You light up, you're filled with energy, and you can't wait to act. With inspiration, what you normally view as work and drudgery becomes joy and pleasure. This is why inspiration is enormously empowering.

Develop Exponential Power

"Inspiration is aliveness in relationship to a goal."

- MARIA VICTORIA PEÑAFLOR MARTINOFF

Develop Exponential Power

The Power of

INTEGRITY

"Without integrity nothing works."

- WERNER ERHARD

One of the most powerful tools I've ever encountered in my efforts to develop and train myself is the notion of integrity as defined by Werner Erhard, founder of EST and Landmark Education.

At the simplest level, Werner defines having integrity as simply doing what you said you would do, the way it was meant to be done or better, and by when you said you would do it. And when you realize that you're not going to get something done, or done on time, integrity involves informing the people who'll be affected right away—with an intention to address the impact on them.

Develop Exponential Power

The benefit of integrity defined this way is mind-bogglingly simple. As Werner puts it, it just makes things work.

One example of how integrity makes things work comes from an experience I had a few years ago when we conducted a workshop in Japan with my former colleague Jerry.

After Jerry and I were done with our preparations, we decided to do some sightseeing and visit Odawara Castle. To get to the Castle, we needed to take a shuttle bus from our hotel to the train station down the hill and then take the train the rest of the way to the site.

The first thing I noticed when I looked at the hotel's notice board was that the shuttle's first trip to the train station was scheduled to leave at *10:12* am—not 10:00am or 10:15am, which I would have expected, but *10:12*am.

And sure enough, when Jerry and I got settled on the shuttle, we noticed a large digital clock on the inside of the shuttle above the door, and at *exactly* 10:11am and 59seconds, the door of the shuttle shut and there was probably nothing that would have stopped it. And we set off for the train station. I felt that if I had come running at that moment, the shuttle bus driver would not have opened the door for me. Sounds cruel? But wait, there is more to it…

When we got to the station down the hill not far from the ocean, it was our first time ever at a Japanese train station. We experienced a slight delay as we had to ask

Develop Exponential Power

for help with the ticket machine. Because of this, we arrived at the platform just a few seconds late. As we came rushing down the stairs to the departure platform, we were about halfway when we saw our train shutting its doors and going on its way.

And that was how I found things to be in Japan for the rest of my trip: everything was timed to start at a precise moment, and there was no waiting or delaying for people who didn't show up at the precise moment.

The logic of this is self-evident. For instance, once there's a delay in the schedule of just one train, it impacts the schedule of countless other trains, causing further and bigger delays along the line. Hence, waiting for just one tardy passenger can hold up hundreds, and potentially even thousands, of other people.

So integrity at this really simple level—the level of just being on time for a shuttle or a train—already goes a tremendous way in making things work. If you look at the countries in the world that are more successful than others, a lot of their success boils down to just having integrity: people stopping at red lights, people throwing their garbage in rubbish bins, people paying their taxes on time, or just paying their taxes.

And integrity is not as complicated or as daunting as it looks. People spend a lot of time and energy justifying why they didn't get things done or why they didn't get them done on time. In my experience, it usually takes far less time and energy just doing the thing as opposed to justifying why it wasn't done.

Develop Exponential Power

For instance, instead of complaining all the time about how getting stuck in traffic makes you late for your meetings, grab an audio book instead and just leave thirty minutes earlier than usual. You'll be on time, you won't be upset, and you'll have learned something new!

The same thing applies to that leak you want to fix, that book you want to write, and those five pounds you want to lose. The point is: if you say you're going to do it, just go ahead and do it. Not only will it increase your productivity, it will boost your confidence and your peace of mind as well.

In short, try integrity. It really works. Where there is integrity there is power. Where there is no integrity there is no power. No power no success.

EXERCISE

Let's work on something simple that many people find quite difficult. It's the same thing I gave as an example earlier in this chapter, which is integrity with time.

This is the exercise: be on time—for *everything*. Be on time for your appointments at home, for your appointments at work, and even for appointments with yourself. If you say you'll be up at 5:00am to go running, be up at 5:00am to go running. If you tell your wife you're picking her up at 6:00pm to go on a date, be at her office by 5:55pm to pick her up for your date. If you tell your son you'll be at his game by 7:00am, then be at his game by 6:55am.

Develop Exponential Power

I kid you not: the greater the percentage of time that you're on time, or better yet a little early for your appointments, the more people (including yourself) will trust and respect you. It seems like a really small thing, but it goes a really, really long way.

"Real integrity is doing the right thing, knowing that nobody's going to know whether you did it or not."

- OPRAH WINFREY

Develop Exponential Power

Develop Exponential Power

The Power of
INTERPRETATION

*"Things don't change.
You change your way of looking, that's all."*

- CARLOS CASTAÑEDA

People often think of interpretation as a very deliberate action. What I mean to say by that is that people tend to believe that they only "interpret" things when they're required to do so by particular circumstances, like when they have to make sense of an abstract work of art or figure out what's happening in a confusing situation.

However, what most people don't realize is that the act of interpretation is automatic and ongoing—in other words, we're *always* interpreting things even if we're not making an effort. It's important for us to really get

Develop Exponential Power

this because our interpretations have a direct impact on our experience of life.

Let me give an example:

My friend Angie was walking in the mall when a good-looking man rushed by and bumped her hard on the shoulder. Because the impact was quite severe, Angie's first impulse was to yell out: "Watch where you're going, you @#(!& !"

Now if you pay attention to what Angie was tempted to say, it's the logical thing to do *if* your interpretation of the incident is: "I got hit because there was an imbecile who wasn't paying attention to where he was going."

But I asked Angie later on, Was this the only possible interpretation of this scenario? As Angie grudgingly admitted, there were *lots* of other ways to look at what happened, such as:

- ☐ he was running after his little boy who wandered away

- ☐ somebody got hurt and he was rushing off to help

- ☐ his parking meter was about to expire

- ☐ he got a bad case of the stomach cramps and needed to reach the toilet in time

- ☐ he thought Angie was cute and just wanted to get her attention

Develop Exponential Power

If you consider each of the interpretations above, you'll notice that each one results in a different emotional response. In the interpretation where the man is rushing off to help, for instance, you would probably feel admiration. In the interpretation where he has a bad case of the stomach cramps, you would probably feel sympathy. And in the interpretation where he wants to get Angie's attention, you would probably feel flattered (if you were in Angie's shoes) or amused (if you were in mine).

The point is, interpretations play a powerful role in our experience of life, like I said earlier, and we make interpretations like Angie's *all of the time*—interpretations that anger, annoy, frustrate, irritate, offend, or depress us.

The worst part is, our initial interpretations might not even be accurate. They rarely are. How many of us have experienced disliking a person at first sight because they dressed or talked in a certain way, and then discovering later that they were really quite likeable?

We can't prevent many of the things that life throws at us, in the same way that Angie couldn't have prevented that man from running into her, but we do have a say about how events in life *affect* us by paying attention to the interpretations we make of these events. Since we can't validate which of our possible interpretations is more accurate in a lot of cases *anyway*, it would be best if we used that "freedom" as the space to choose interpretations that are empowering versus disempowering.

Develop Exponential Power

For instance, Angie never got to find out if the man who bumped into her really was just being careless or really just needed to handle an emergency. But guess which interpretation is likelier to leave her at peace?

For me, at least, the choice seems pretty obvious.

The bottom-line is: don't allow your interpretations to rob you of your power. Since they're *your* interpretations anyway, you might as well choose the ones that leave you empowered.

> "If you are troubled by external circumstances, it is not the circumstances that trouble you, but your own perception of them and they are within your power to change at any time ...."
>
> - MARCUS AURELIUS

EXERCISE

Pick something that happened to you in the last week that left you feeling very upset. It can be a major thing like a setback at work or a minor thing like getting held up in traffic. Whatever the event is, list down *at least* ten different interpretations of it.

Now, this can be very difficult at first—especially if you're absolutely convinced that your assessment of things *is* the right assessment. (Have you noticed that you're always right, by the way?) But if you persist in this exercise and really take it seriously, you'll begin to realize that each interpretation you come up with is really *just* that: an interpretation.

Of course, some interpretations might be more far-fetched than others, but I'm certain that you'll also come up with interpretations that are *as* plausible as your initial assessment *without* being as disempowering.

As you do this exercise, you might even begin to realize something else: the likelier you are to believe in a given interpretation, the higher your chances are of finding evidence to support it!

Here's something else I encourage you to try while doing this exercise, which is to pay attention to the emotional response that each interpretation generates.

Every interpretation results in a different emotion: some are positive, some are negative, and some are neutral. Allow yourself to fully feel the emotion that comes with each interpretation. At the end of the exercise, ask yourself: "Which of these emotions would I rather feel more often in my life?"

And once you've answered that, ask yourself: "What kinds of interpretation tend to result in these kinds of emotion?"

In answering this question, you'll have discovered for yourself a powerful and effective means of altering your experience of life *without* having to worry about controlling external events.

Develop Exponential Power

"Change your thinking, your interpretation of the world, change the way you see! To change the way you see is to change the world."

- JEAN-YVES LELOUP

Develop Exponential Power

The Power of

LUCK

"Be prepared, work hard, and hope for a little luck. Recognize that the harder you work and the better prepared you are, the more luck you might have."

ED BRADLEY

When I ask people what they think luck is, what I often hear them say is:

"It' something I wish I had more of."

"It's one of those good things that you can never expect."

"It's a superstition."

In other words, people tend to think of luck as a positive yet uncontrollable and unpredictable occurrence—something that you can pray for or wish for but never really expect.

Develop Exponential Power

However, I have a different view of luck, which is that luck is simply the intersection of opportunity and preparation.

I'll say that again: luck is what happens when a person creates and prepares for the opportunities they want.

Let me share a personal example. I've been wanting to write this book (yes, this book that you're holding in your hands) for 10 years. But it didn't happen during those 10 years simply because I wasn't preparing for it to happen and I wasn't creating opportunities for it to happen. I wasn't creating an outline, or taking down notes, or even telling people that I was interested in writing a book!

Then the day came when I finally told myself: Alright Bjorn, you're going to get that book written *this* year. The next thing I knew, I was at a juice bar chatting with a friend when she casually mentioned being a freelance editor. I immediately said: "Really? Well, I happen to need an editor who can help me write my book!"

Just like that, I got the resource I needed to do something I'd wanted to do for a decade! Some people would call it luck, but it happened simply because I was finally prepared and I was alert to any opportunities coming my way.

And like I mentioned earlier, opportunities *can* be created—you don't even need to wait for them to happen.

Develop Exponential Power

For instance, people who say they want a romantic relationship often act as if their ideal partner were simply going to drop out of the sky and onto their lap. But if you want to end up with someone, you need to create opportunities to *meet* people first. That means going out, making friends, joining clubs—maybe even posting something online! Of course, you can *wait* for the opportunity instead of creating it, but you need to be ready to wait for a quite possibly long, long time.

And you don't just create the opportunities, you prepare for them too. In the context of dating, this means always being well-dressed and always being well-groomed, among other things. After all, you don't want to meet the man or woman of your dreams for the first time and spoil the occasion by looking like something the cat dragged in.

So yes, luck *can* happen by accident, but if you look closely, the "luckiest" individuals—and the most powerful ones—are the people who create opportunities and prepare for them rather than wait for them and get caught by surprise.

EXERCISE

Pick an area in your life where you want to be "lucky." It can be the area of your career, the area of your finances, or the area of your relationships.

Then on a sheet of paper, create two columns. In the column on the left, list down all the *opportunities* you

Develop Exponential Power

can create for yourself in this area. For instance, if it involves your finances, opportunities you can write down can include: getting promoted at work, getting the chance to set up a side business, and so on and so forth.

Then in the column on the right, list down all the ways you can think of to *prepare* for the opportunities you listed down in the column on the left. To go back to our earlier example, next to getting the chance to set up a side business, for instance, you can write down: learning how to manage a business, finding potential investors, and so on and so forth.

The final part of the exercise is for you to follow through on the ways of preparing that you listed down in the column on the right. So if you wrote down "learning how to manage a business," following through means signing up for a business management course, reading a book, or getting the guidance of an expert.

I promise you, when you undertake this exercise faithfully, your luck—and along with it your power—will expand by leaps and bounds.

""I'm a great believer in luck, and I find the harder I work, the more I have of it."

Develop Exponential Power

- THOMAS JEFFERSON

"Luck is when opportunity and preparation intersect."

- BJORN MARTINOFF

Develop Exponential Power

Develop Exponential Power

The Power of

PEACE

"Peace is not merely a distant goal that we seek, but a means by which we arrive at that goal."

- MARTIN LUTHER KING, JR.

In the chapter on ALIGNMENT, I talked about how conflicts with other people or within ourselves can lead to a lot of wasted time, energy, and effort. This is because conflicts cancel our energies out: either someone's effort opposes ours, or our own self-doubts paralyze or delay us.

In this chapter on PEACE, I'm going to talk about a different kind of conflict that weighs us down: not the conflict that comes from two agendas or two values countering each other, but the conflict that comes from not being at peace with ourselves because of guilt or regret.

Now, I'm a Roman Catholic by birth and upbringing, so I grew up being familiar with the notion of confession. For a long time though, I didn't understand the nature and purpose of the sacrament of confession. Things started getting clearer for me when I started to study different philosophical and religious systems. In the course of my research, I came across the Church of Scientology's system for dealing with what it calls "overts" (harmful actions) and "withholds" (harmful actions that we conceal). The process is similar to what you would go through in Catholic confession—the main difference is in the framework used for assessing what it is that you actually "confess." The Catholic Church, for instance, would ask you to assess where you failed in terms of the Seven Sins or the Ten Commandments, whereas the Church of Scientology would ask you to assess yourself in terms of offenses against your family, offenses against your group, offenses against mankind, and so on and so forth.

The point is, when I went through the process, I started feeling incredibly *lighter*. And the impact wasn't confined to my psychological or spiritual well-being. The peace of mind I got as a result of the process literally allowed me to triple my sales results!

This might seem really strange to you at first, especially if you're used to separating the different areas of your life the way most people do. But what many people don't realize is that our feelings of guilt and regret about different things accumulate over the years and leave us carrying an increasingly heavier burden. We might not even be aware that we have such feelings, or when we are aware of them, we might not even take them seriously. But I assert that these feelings of guilt and regret *are* there and that they *do* have an impact. It's as if you're spending your life trying to win a hundred meter sprint not knowing that you're carrying a forty kilo weight on your back! Good luck with winning that race—it's simply not going to happen.

So whether you're a Catholic or a Scientologist or a believer of some other faith or even a non-believer, I suggest that you find a process that will allow you to get present to all the things you've held on to—all the things that we call "baggage" for very good reason—and begin letting them go. The healing and lightness you'll find as a result will be enormously rewarding in their own right. The fact that they'll also empower you in the other areas of your life just happens to be a really big bonus.

EXERCISE

Take some time to sit down and start listing all the things in your life that you feel guilty about or that you regret doing or that you regret not doing. List down *anything* and *everything* for which you blame yourself, resent yourself, or hold against yourself. List down all the perceived errors, failures, flaws, missed opportunities, mistakes, and shortcomings. List everything down: when these incidents happened, where they happened, what their impact was on you and on other people, and what you could have done differently to handle the situation.

The point of this exercise is to allow you to literally purge yourself of all this baggage and negative energy by "confessing" or acknowledging to yourself what didn't work in your life. But by also having you look at what you could have done differently, the exercise is designed to leave you with power the next time you come across a similar situation. This way, you're not trapped by what happened in the past. Rather, the past becomes a guide to a more powerful future. You can then start the process of letting go.

Because if you think about it, what's happened has happened—there's no changing the past—and your guilt and regret will only poison your present and your future. Start to notice instead how all the "errors," "failures," "flaws," "mistakes," and "shortcomings" actually taught you things, built your character, made you a stronger person and brought you to where you are today. Start to acknowledge yourself for having done the best that you could have done in those past situations given the state of your knowledge and ability at those times. The point is: do what needs to be done so that you can be at peace with yourself, your past, and the totality of your life.

Now, this is an enormously difficult exercise to do, and it's likely it will take several sessions. Take as long as you need and be patient with yourself. There are some things you won't want to remember and there are some things that will take a long time for you to remember.

Develop Exponential Power

But you'll notice that as you keep going at it, you'll feel lighter and lighter, as if a burden that you never even knew existed was slowly being lifted. And when that weight is gone, all your attention and energy can now go into powerfully creating your present and your future.

""There is no way to peace, peace is the way."

A. J. MUSTE

Develop Exponential Power

The Power of PRESENCE

"The most precious gift we can offer others is our presence. When mindfulness embraces those we love, they will bloom like flowers."

THICH NHAT HANH

When people talk about presence in the sense of having "presence of mind," they usually refer to someone's ability to masterfully handle an emergency.

What I find strange about this is that there's somehow an assumption that we only need our minds to be fully present whenever there's a crisis. In most other situations, it seems as if it's okay if we're not really paying attention to what's going on.

Develop Exponential Power

I'm going to assert, however, that part of being powerful is being able to be fully present—to have full presence of mind—on an ongoing basis. Buddhism recognizes this, which is why it says that "mindfulness," or the state of being attentively aware of reality in the current moment, is the seventh element of the eightfold path to enlightenment.

The reason why being present is so critical to power is very simple: unless you really know what's going on, how can you effectively deal with any situation? And if you're not fully paying attention to things, how can you really know what's going on?

In other words, power depends on an accurate assessment of the situation, and an accurate assessment of the situation depends on close observation. So if you want to have power in any situation, start by being present. (I talk about something similar in the chapter on REALITY.)

The problem, however, is that we're not used to being present. In fact, it's not just that we're unused to being present—it's more like we're almost never present at all!

The reason for this is that our attention is always diverted by the constant chatter in our heads. This chatter is made up of all the thoughts and feelings and assessments and reactions and judgments and opinions that are always going on in our skulls. We're often so busy paying attention to all these internal rackets that we hardly have any attention left for what's going on

Develop Exponential Power

outside. We function instead by going on auto-pilot—by letting mindless routines take over.

You'll know what I mean if you think about how you are when you're driving. When you're driving, haven't you noticed that your mind usually wanders off to the meeting that you've got on your schedule, or to the food that you're having for lunch, or to the gift that you need to buy your wife, or to the appointment that you might miss . . . and so on and so forth? Very rarely are you fully paying attention to the act of driving, to what's on the road ahead of you or to the buildings that are flashing by outside your car. Given how absent your mind usually is when you drive, the only thing that will prevent you from getting into an accident is the speediness of your reflexes (so hopefully they're very fast!).

In my case, one area where I find myself not being present on occasion is when I'm coaching people! Sometimes, my thoughts will go somewhere else: I'll be anticipating the next question, or formulating my next answer, or worrying about how much money I'll make or how many more clients I'll get from the engagement. Sometimes, I'll go back to being present only to discover that it's my client who's not present!

That's why in my coaching engagements, one of the very first things I teach my clients is how to be present. Because if their mind or if my mind is somewhere else, no coaching will take place. They'll be saying something and I'll miss it, or I'll be saying something and they'll miss it. Or they might be saying something and intending something else, and I'll miss *that*. The point is, just like in

Develop Exponential Power

any other situation in life, effectiveness and power in a coaching relationship depend on the parties' abilities to be present.

So if power depends on being present, and being present depends on being able to pay attention to things other than the constant chatter in our heads, then we start developing power by learning how *not* to be distracted by the noise in our heads. And this is precisely what you'll get to do in the exercise below.

EXERCISE

It's important to know before you start this exercise that the noise in your head will never go away. You can't control your thoughts and you can't control your feelings. But the point of this exercise is not to stop the noise, but rather, to stop being distracted by it so that you can pay attention to other things for a change (like reality, for instance).

One method I've discovered that really works for me is to tell the voices in my head to "Go sit in the corner and have an ice cream and I'll come and get you when I'm done with what I'm doing." (This is very similar to a method I share in the chapter on COURAGE.)

Why this works is because it's very gentle and very lighthearted and there's no force or threat behind it. A variation that I also find very effective is to tell the voices in my head that "I really appreciate your inputs and I'll take them into account, but now I really need to focus." This works by acknowledging the reason why there are all those voices in your head to begin with—which is to fulfill your intentions in the best way they know how. Have you noticed that the chatter is always about the things that matter to you?

So just to be clear, it's not that the noise in your head is bad, it's just that it gets in the way of your being present.

Just one final note: it might seem a little strange to talk to yourself this way, but believe me, it works. The only thing I caution you to do is to not talk to yourself out loud!

OPTIONAL EXERCISE

This is an exercise you can do if you want to specifically develop an ability to be present to other people. It will involve other people though—or one other person at the very least.

First, find someone who's willing to be your partner for this exercise. Then find a place where you won't be interrupted and face each other (preferably standing up) and look into each other's eyes.

Stay like this for at least three minutes.

Now, this is surprisingly difficult for a lot of people. In my coaching engagements, I've seen people daydream, fidget, giggle, laugh, look away, make faces, and zone out—anything just to avoid having to be fully present to the other person!

Develop Exponential Power

So do this exercise fully and do it as often as necessary until you find yourself actually being present to the other person.

And then see what that provides you in your life.

Develop Exponential Power

> *"As we let our light shine, we unconsciously give other people permission to do the same. As we are liberated from our own fear, our presence actually liberates others."*
>
> MARIANNE WILLIAMSON

Develop Exponential Power

The Power of PUROSE

"Start with the end in mind."

STEPHEN COVEY

On the broadest terms, purpose can be defined as the reason for which something exists. In my work as an executive coach, one of the things that really fascinate me is how organizations are so much more effective than individuals when it comes to articulating their purpose.

What do I mean?

Well, look at any organization. It can be the company you work for, or the charity you support, or the church you attend. I'm very sure that all of these will have a mission statement somewhere that includes a very clear and concise description of what the organization does, or it will have a purpose giving it a reason for existence.

But if you ask the people you know what their purpose is, chances are that they won't be able to tell you. Or, if they can tell you, it won't be a very clear, concise and consistent answer.

I think the reason why organizations are better than individuals when it comes to articulating their purpose is because organizations are deliberate creations. That is, all organizations are born with a specific objective in mind. Companies are born because a person or a group of people have an objective to make a certain amount of money or to sell a particular kind of product or service. Non-profit organizations are born because a person has an objective to address a certain kind of social need. Social networks are born because people have an objective to remain connected with other people who have similar needs or interests.

In other words, organizations only come into being because people use them to fulfill certain intentions. These intentions can automatically serve as the purpose of the organization.

With people, on the other hand, it's different. None of us asked to be born. None of us came into being with a clear and definite idea of the purpose for which we were born. So unlike organizations that have intentions that are clear from the outset, human beings don't come with "automatic" intentions that can serve as guidelines for how we should live.

Develop Exponential Power

And this is okay when we're just starting out. When we're young, we don't have to worry about having a purpose yet. There's all that growing up and studying that needs to be done.

But once we reach a certain age and we're on our own, then having a purpose becomes absolutely critical.

Why?

Because without a purpose, we can easily spend the rest of our lives just running on auto-pilot, doing what our family wants or what society wants without really fulfilling a deeper or more meaningful intention. It's not that there's anything wrong with this, it's just that in my experience, people who live on auto-pilot don't live very happy lives. There's always a sense that "there's something missing" and that "there has to be more to life than this." It seems that people living without a purpose seem to be just floating along on the river of life. But when you think of it, even a dead fish can float along the river.

And, while having a purpose is absolutely critical to living a happy and fulfilling life, it's not always easy to discover or create a purpose. Some people are fortunate to find, very early in life, what it is that they were "born to do." Other people can spend years—even decades—on the search.

In my case, finding my purpose was a process that happened over several years. I knew that I'd finally found it when I created a statement of purpose that inspired me every time I read it or recalled it. Just thinking about the statement was enough to excite me and energize me. The purpose statement I created was: "To be a trusted advisor to world leaders."

I created that statement 10 years ago, and since then my life has been nothing short of *amazing*. Creating that purpose gave me something to wake up for, to take action for, and to look forward to. It gave me a sense of focus and direction. It gave me a WHY!

Before I created my purpose, I didn't know what to focus my life on: I was scattering my time and energy studying and learning different things without being clear on what exactly I was preparing myself for. When I discovered my purpose, it really funneled my time, energy, and attention. Suddenly, I knew what kind of books to read, what kinds of people to meet, and what kinds of skills to develop.

The other benefit of discovering my purpose, besides simplifying and focusing my life, was that it provided me inspiration. I created my purpose 10 years ago, and even when I had fulfilled it on several different levels already, it still inspired me and I still continue to see new ways of expressing it in the world.

So whether it comes to you easily or not, finding your purpose is something that's a matter of urgency, because unless you're clear about your purpose in life, you'll be scattering your time, energy, and attention on different activities and in different directions. It's like being in a foreign city for the first time and not knowing what you want to accomplish as a tourist. Chances are, you'll spend hours just wandering around aimlessly, doing a little window shopping here and some sightseeing there, following the trail of some tourist groups here and following the trail of some locals there. In the end, you'll be tired and exhausted and you won't even have seen the best of what the city has to offer. On the other hand, if you were clear that your purpose was "to see the best museums and to eat the finest food in Paris," then a day-long itinerary would involve visiting the top three museums and the top three restaurants in Paris. There's no wasting time or squandering money wandering around alleys or visiting churches or boating down rivers. It's museums and restaurants and that's it. Not that there's anything wrong with churches. I love churches and temples and any other house of God. But let's get back to what we're discussing here... PURPOSE.

The same principle of having purpose applies to our lives—more so, in fact. We only have a limited amount of time on this earth, and if we want it to count for something, then we have to get clear about what we want to accomplish during the time that we have.

Some of you might be thinking: "But I really don't know what I want!"

If that's what's there for you, don't worry: you're not alone. The good news is that even if you can't think of a purpose for yourself, there are many things in your life that can *point* towards a possible purpose.

The first place to look at is all the things that you like doing or enjoy doing. The things that inspire and fulfill you are the biggest clues to what your purpose could be.

Develop Exponential Power

You might be good at doing something, but if it doesn't inspire or fulfill you, chances are it's not your purpose.

Remember, your purpose is the reason for which you exist. An inspiring purpose is incredibly fulfilling and amazingly motivating. So a good question to ask yourself when you're creating your purpose is: "What reason would be worth living for, or what reason would be worthy of my existence? Or what would be worth spending the rest of my life on? Or how would I want to be remembered at my 80th birthday? What kind of being or accomplishment would I be remembered for?"

The answers to these questions will lead you to your true purpose. And often the answers may not be an accomplishment at all. Sometimes it could be a way of being.

But what's the relationship between purpose and power? What does purpose have to do with power?

First of all, just having a purpose is enormously empowering, fulfilling, and motivating. Knowing what your life is about provides a tremendous amount of inspiration and motivation. When you're clear about your purpose, you can metaphorically, and even literally, move mountains.

Second, having a purpose allows you to focus all your time, energy, and attention. Like I mentioned earlier, it serves as a guide for the choices you make and the actions you take, commitments you accept, and even people you surround yourself with. In other words, having a purpose makes life *simple*—and that simplicity provides a lot of clarity, and with that clarity comes power.

A final word about purpose: once you have one, it's important to keep reminding yourself of it. In the same way that organizations put up copies of their purpose or mission on their office walls, it's advisable that you put a copy of your purpose somewhere where you can easily see it. That way, you can remind yourself time and again of what it is that your life is about.

EXERCISE

If you don't have a purpose yet, this is the time for you to create one. If you're not sure about what your purpose could be, start by listing down all the things that inspire you or fulfill you or that you enjoy doing. List everything down in a notebook. The list can be as long as you like. Don't censor yourself. Don't worry at this point about how the different things or activities you enjoy seem to be contradicting another. Right now, what's important is that you get in touch with ALL that inspires or fulfills you.

Give yourself a week to work on this list because you might think of new things as the days go on.

After a week, review your entire list and start looking for themes. Do many of the items on your list have some logical connection to each other? Do many things seem to repeat themselves? For instance, one theme you might find is creativity: you like painting and writing

Develop Exponential Power

and being creative with your hands. Another theme you might find is sociability: you like going to parties and getting to know people and keeping them connected. Rearrange your list so that the items are clustered around one or a few of these themes.

Once you've rearranged your list, examine it again. Is it possible that the themes you've come up with (if you have more than one) have an even deeper logical connection between them? Try to see if it's possible to unite all these themes into one over-arching purpose.

If you can't find a single over-arching purpose, then try to see which of the themes is most important to you. This theme may very well be your purpose. It doesn't mean that you now have to get rid of all the other themes—it just means that you could be prioritizing your time according to how important the themes are to you.

Once you have this "draft" purpose, test it. Put it up for a month and during that month, see if living your life by this purpose provides you with power, passion, simplicity, and inspiration.

If it doesn't, it doesn't mean that you've failed—it just means that there's something that needs to be tweaked, or fine-tuned or further looked into. If it does, then congratulations! You are now living a life of purpose—a powerful life.

A Note to those in organizations:

Develop Exponential Power

From my experience and my work with the world's largest organizations, I have found it to be one hundred times more powerful and inspiring to have a purpose than a mission.

A mission in its purest sense is just a statement of what the organization does. A purpose is a statement of why it does it. Disney's mission could have been to provide entertainment for the masses, but Disney didn't choose to have a mission. Instead Disney chose a powerful purpose. The Purpose that Disney chose was "To make people happy." Now it doesn't matter if I am a manager at Disney, or a cashier, or the person scrubbing the toilet because I can be inspired to get out of bed in the morning because despite of what I am DOING, my real work is to make people happy! And for that, even I can gratefully scrub a toilet, or be a cashier, or sweep the street. Because it's not what I am doing. It's about what I am creating. Happiness.

> "You and I want our lives to matter. We want our lives to make a real difference – to be of genuine consequence in the world. We know that there is no satisfaction in merely going through the motions, even if those motions make us successful or even if we have arranged to make those motions pleasant. We want to know we have had some impact on the world. In fact, you and I want to contribute to the quality of life. We want to make the world work."
>
> WERNER ERHARD

Develop Exponential Power

The Power of

REALITY

"Common sense is the knack of seeing things as they are, and doing things as they ought to be done."

C.E. STOWE

Few people live in reality. What I mean to say by that is that few people, very few people in fact, are actually in touch with what's really the case with things—with what's really going on.

A lot of this has to do with something I talked about in the chapter on INTERPRETATION, which is that we automatically look at things in a certain way instead of as how they really are. For instance, people living in Manila will look out of their window and see the rain, and instead of seeing the rain as "water literally falling down from the sky," what they'll see instead is "lots and LOTS of horrendous traffic jams."

Now in the chapter on INTERPRETATION, I talked about the power that comes from being able to choose our interpretation of reality. In this chapter, I'm going to focus on the power that comes from just confronting reality itself—the power, in other words, that comes from being able to see rain as rain and not as traffic or inconvenience or floods or colds.

Why there's power in seeing reality as it is is because we can then focus all our attention and energy on addressing it directly rather than getting distracted or disempowered by all our interpretations.

The Japanese, for instance, live in one of the most seismic regions of the world. Possible interpretations of this fact are "it's dangerous to live in Japan" or "you can't build high-rise buildings in Japan." The Japanese, however, have simply confronted the reality of their geography as it is—which is that it's earthquake-prone—and have accordingly developed the most advanced earthquake-resistance technologies in the world (while continuing to build many spectacular high-rise buildings).

At the same time, the Japanese have also suffered from not confronting reality as it is. The meltdown of the Fukushima Daiichi Nuclear Power Plant following the damage caused by the March 2011 Tōhoku earthquake and tsunami could have been avoided if the Tokyo Electric Power Company had heeded the warnings given by the United States Nuclear Regulatory Commission as

Develop Exponential Power

early as 1990. The Fukushima disaster is currently the largest nuclear accident in history since the 1986 Chernobyl disaster and experts have estimated that it could take hundreds and potentially thousands of workers *decades* to clean up the effects of the meltdown.

As you see from the examples I just gave, there's tremendous power in being able to see reality just as it is and then acting accordingly.

To go back to my earlier example, the Philippines is a tropical country and constant rain is therefore a reality in the country. And because the rain does seem to cause more traffic jams, traffic jams are therefore also a reality in the country.

At first, this was something I complained about along with everyone else. But when I realized that the traffic jams, like the rain, are just how things *are* in the Philippines, at least right now, I decided to address that reality directly rather than waste my time and energy in grumbling about it.

So what I did was I started listening to audio books in my car. I figured that if I was going to be spending a lot of time on the road, I could use that time very productively by using it as an opportunity to learn something new. Since then, my "reading" has stepped up from just one book a month (which was the average before I started listening to audio books) to up to two books a week!

Now, it's not an exaggeration for me to say that I actually enjoy my time on the road, because it's my time to learn something new for myself. But this is something I would never have come up with if I hadn't confronted and accepted reality just the way it is.

EXERCISE

One area in life where I've consistently noticed people not dealing with reality is the area of their personal appearance. For example, cosmetic surgeons have reported that many patients still feel the same way about how they look even after they've had drastic adjustments made. So given that this is a particularly challenging area, I'm going to pick it as the area to focus on for this exercise.

The exercise consists of this: everyday, ideally several times in a day, look at yourself in the mirror. Plant yourself in front of a mirror in an undisturbed place and get present to every detail of your face. Do this without squirming, without sighing, without flinching, and without giving in to all the thoughts that automatically run through your head whenever you look in a mirror—thoughts like my nose is too big, my lips are too thin, my skin is too dull . . . and so on and so forth.

It's very likely that before this exercise, you've never taken a frank, straight look at your own face. Keep doing this until you get to the point where you can see your face and just see your face. And then see what that does for you.

Develop Exponential Power

""The truth is not found in a different set of circumstances. The truth is always and only found in the circumstances you've got."

WERNER ERHARD

Develop Exponential Power

The Power of RESPONSIBILITY

"Take your life in your own hands, and what happens? A terrible thing: no one to blame."

ERICA JONG

One of the standard dictionary definitions of responsibility is that it's the state of being accountable or "blame-able" for something.

Now most people understand what responsibility is, but I would also assert that most people don't understand how large the scope of their responsibility is. What I mean to say by that is that people generally limit their responsibility to things that they consciously choose. For example: "I chose to marry this person, so I am therefore responsible for my marriage to this person," or "I chose to have children, so I am therefore responsible for properly raising these children."

Most people, however, never consider themselves responsible for things they didn't consciously choose.

Develop Exponential Power

For example, I spent a good part of my life dealing with a father who often told me that I wouldn't make it, that I'd never succeed and that I'd never amount to anything. I resented my dad because of this and spent many years blaming him for what I felt was my mediocre life. I never chose my dad—he was the dad I got—and I never chose the way he treated me. Therefore, I couldn't be held responsible for him and for the effects he had on me and my life.

Then one day, I heard my friend Anthony Robbins share the following story:

Once while the Buddha was traveling with his followers, a man who didn't like him started following him as well. The man would challenge the Buddha at every opportunity he got: attacking him, criticizing him, and insulting him. This went on for days and weeks and months, until finally, the man approached the Buddha and said:

"I've been following you for months and I've attacked and criticized and insulted you at every chance I've found. But not once did you get affected by anything I said. 'Why not?'"

The Buddha replied:

"May I ask you a question?"

The man nodded.

So the Buddha went on: "If someone offers you a gift and you do not accept it, to whom then does the gift belong?"

Develop Exponential Power

The man responded:

"It belongs to the person giving the gift."

The Buddha replied:

"Precisely, so when someone gives you an insult, a challenge, or a criticism and you do not accept it, to whom then does it belong?"

The man was silent, walked away and was never heard from again.

When I heard this story from Tony, I realized that even if I hadn't chosen my dad and even if I hadn't chosen how he looked at me, what I had chosen—without realizing it—was to accept his view of me. Just like me, the Buddha had never chosen the company of that man, and he hadn't chosen that man's dislike for him—but he did choose whether to accept that man's attacks or not.

It was in that moment that I understood how you can actually be responsible for everything in your life, even if there are many things in your life that you never consciously chose. By assuming responsibility for the entirety of your life, you take back and return to yourself the power that circumstances would otherwise have in determining your happiness and fulfillment. Whenever you take responsibility for something, blame disappears—and power emerges. As it turns out, both blaming and taking responsibility are habits. Blaming is the habit of victims, while taking responsibility is a habit of winners.

EXERCISE

Look into your life and see what "gifts" life has given you that you've accepted, consciously or otherwise. Make a list and see which of these "gifts" you really want in your life and which ones you want to send back.

How do you send "gifts" back? Simple: you choose not to accept them. There's nothing else you have to do. Notice that the Buddha didn't blame the man for being who he was, and he certainly didn't blame himself for having somehow allowed the man into in his life. He simply took responsibility by not accepting an unwanted gift.

OPTIONAL EXERCISE

Whenever you find yourself blaming someone or something or feeling disempowered, helpless, and weak, sit down and start brainstorming on the ways that you can be the "cause" of the situation.

Now, don't do this just so that you can shift the blame onto yourself! This is not about shifting blame but about making it disappear altogether.

The point of looking for ways that you can be the "cause" of the situation is so that you can then look for ways to actually DO something about the situation. Simply adopting the point of view of a powerless victim will do nothing except leave you being exactly that: POWERLESS.

Develop Exponential Power

When you accept responsibility, you take on being the cause in the matter. When you are the cause in having created the situation, then you can also un-create that situation. You can now truly be the Master of life as you experience it. You can now truly transform the experience of your life because you have now become the Master of your Destiny.

> *""Let everyone sweep in front of his own door, and the whole world will be clean."*
>
> JOHANN WOLFGANG VON GOETHE

Develop Exponential Power

Develop Exponential Power

The Power of

TRUST

"You may be deceived if you trust too much, but you will live in torment if you do not trust enough."

FRANK CRANE

In my experience as a trainer and coach to senior executive teams, the one thing that's usually missing the most is trust among colleagues. I've witnessed many instances where relationships have deteriorated so much that executives on the same team have stopped talking to each other for as long as two or even three years! In these cases, restoring trust among team members has the single greatest effect on boosting the level of their performance.

Develop Exponential Power

Trust is a function of integrity and authenticity (both of which we cover in a different chapters) but it can also be enhanced in other ways.

One of the most effective tools that I've discovered is what L. Ron Hubbard calls the ARC Triangle. Hubbard is known more famously as the founder of the Church of Scientology, and while his life may have attracted a lot of controversy, some of the tools that he developed—including the ARC Triangle—have proven to be remarkably robust.

The letters A, R, and C in the ARC Triangle refer to *affinity*, *reality* and *communication*. Very roughly, *affinity* refers to the affection between people; *reality* to the world that they share; and *communication* to the exchanges between them. According to Hubbard, increasing any one of the three also increases the other two.

For example, if I share my world with someone else more often, the increase in our shared reality will increase the regard we have for each other and the quality of the communication between us. By continuously working on any one of the three, the other two increase accordingly and the increases can quickly build up into a virtuous upward spiral. However, the opposite also holds true. By allowing any one of the three to deteriorate, the other two deteriorate as well. And if the deterioration isn't addressed, a vicious downward spiral can be the result.

What does this have to do with trust? Very simply, when we have high levels of *affinity*, *communication* and shared *reality* between people, we have a solid foundation for building trust among them. Hence, the ARC Triangle provides an immediate and straightforward access to cultivating one of the most essential elements of power, which is simply the element of trust.

For example, one of the areas in my life where I've found applying the ARC Triangle to be very effective is the area of prospecting for clients. In the past, when I would do "cold calls" or "cold emails" to prospective clients, I'd usually just stick to sharing my accomplishments when it came to the part about sharing my credentials. Then when I started applying the ARC Triangle, specifically the part about increasing my shared reality with others, I started saying a little bit more about myself beyond just my achievements. I'd talk a little bit about being a husband or a father or some of my other experiences in life like the movie I saw the night before, or the weather as I experienced it going to work or looking outside of the office window. Just doing this had a tremendous impact on the rate of responses from prospective clients!

And in general I think our business interactions have become very mechanical. When we're working, we relate to other people—and get related to by other people—as an issue to address, an ordeal to survive, a transaction to complete or a signature to collect. Worse we relate to another as machines. When we share something about ourselves that *isn't* related to the work, it actually humanizes the experience. Suddenly, we're not cogs in the machine interacting with other cogs in the machine. People appreciate that injection of warmth and humanity into the interaction and that's why they're likelier to respond.

For me, I not only enjoy the fact that I get more responses. I also enjoy it when other people respond to what I'm sharing by sharing something of themselves as well! That's when things get really fun, interesting, and rewarding.

EXERCISE

Next time you find yourself speaking to a stranger, whether in a personal or professional context, share a little bit about what's going on in your life with him or with her. It doesn't have to be particularly serious or significant—it can be as mundane as the weather, a film you just watched or an incident with your children.

Whatever it is, try sharing more about yourself than usual—and see how the increase in shared reality leads to more affinity, communication and trust with the person to whom you're speaking.

OPTIONAL EXERCISE

Another exercise I recommend is something that I use in my work in coaching executive teams. This exercise typically makes the biggest difference in restoring trust among executive team members.

Develop Exponential Power

As I mentioned earlier in the chapter, one way to increase trust is to increase the shared reality between people—that is, to have people share their perspective of life or of a situation with the people around them. However, there's a way of sharing one's reality that can backfire by actually *increasing* the hostility between people—and that's by sharing one's reality from the perspective of *blaming.*

What this looks like is this: "It's hard for *me* to get *my* job done when *you* never give me clear instructions on time and when *you* keep changing direction . . ." and so on and so forth.

So to actually generate trust when sharing one's reality, it's best to share reality in what I refer to as a constructive, future-based manner. That is, instead of having people share what they don't want or don't like, especially in another person (e.g., "you never take the initiative"), I ask them to share what they *do* like or what they *do* want in another person and to say it in the future tense if necessary (e.g., "you could really increase your effectiveness if you took the lead in the projects you're handling").

The point is that people never like to hear what's wrong with them, even if that feedback is shared with the best of intentions. But people will *always* be interested in hearing how they can be more effective or more successful, and they'll greatly appreciate your contributions in this area. You'll be amazed to see what a simple exercise in sharing reality from a constructive,

Develop Exponential Power

future-based perspective can do for the level of affinity and trust in a team.

Develop Exponential Power

The Power of
VISION

"The pain will push you until the vision pulls you."

Rev. Dr. Michael Bernard Beckwith

When you don't know where you want to end up, it doesn't matter much where you're going or in what direction you're headed. Not having a vision about where we want to go at work or in life almost always ensures you won't get there. Having a clear vision will help you get focused on the outcome and help you attract that outcome.

Develop Exponential Power

When you develop your very first vision, you may think that you are not very daring to have a vision that is really out there, or a vision that truly inspires you. You may not yet have experienced this working for you and may feel cautious, even doubtful about it. This would be the time to let go of those feelings and move yourself toward faith.

A vision can be expressed as a statement or a picture, a collage or a drawing. Most organizations will prefer a written vision statement over a visual representation. Written statements may seem to be more appropriate for the corporate world but they can still be supplemented with a visual created by a team. A visual representation of the vision can help make this vision more real in the minds of the participating members. And because there is a feeling of it being more real, people can already have a taste of what it will be like to achieve that vision, and that in turn motivates them more, making the vision much easier to accomplish.

The most powerful and inspiring vision statements are very specific. They include a time and place, meaning, when and where it will be accomplished. They are almost always a good stretch beyond what we can accomplish. And they are short statements that people can easily remember.

Develop Exponential Power

There is no use for a vision statement that you or your people cannot remember. When working with teams, it is important for everyone to be aligned on the vision. If your people are not aligned and the vision was just developed by the head of the team, the team members may still believe that they are aligned but in their hearts they are not. When your people only buy in on a verbal level, this is called lip service. Meaning they express alignment but in reality are not fully aligned. There are times when your people may even hold the firm belief that they are aligned, but the reality is that it is never as powerful as a vision created as a team.

"Don't ask yourself what the world needs: Ask yourself what makes you come alive. And then go and do that. Because what the world needs is people who have come alive."

- Rev. Dr. HOWARD THURMAN

Develop Exponential Power

"The most common way people give up their power is by thinking they don't have any."

- ALICE WALKER

Develop Exponential Power

The Powers in Brief

The Power of ACTION
Create, Destroy, or Maintain

The Power of ALIGNMENT
How to triple your results without any extra effort

The Power of AUTHENTICITY
How to cut through the smoke screen and get to the bottom line

The Power of BELIEF
How what you believe can bring you to a screeching halt

The Power of CHOICE
How to have a choice when there isn't any

The Power of COMMITMENT
The driving power behind your goals

The Power of CONTRIBUTION
Be energized by making a difference

The Power of COURAGE
Expand then blow apart your limits

The Power of DETACHMENT
Being open to something most often brings it

The Power of EMPATHY

Develop Exponential Power

How to have instant access into someone's world

The Power of FAITH
How to have certainty in uncertain times

The Power of FLEXIBILITY
Getting what you want even when there are obstacles

The Power of FOCUS
Your road sign to your destiny

The Power of FUN
How to have more energy when you need it most

The Power of GRATITUDE
Being thankful gives you more

The Power of GROWTH
If you're not growing you're dying

The Power of HUMILITY
Be humble, be unforgettable

The Power of INSPIRATION
Your heart will pull you forward

The Power of INTEGRITY
Without it nothing works

The Power of INTERPRETATION
How to turn lead into gold

The Power of LUCK
Luck is when opportunity meets preparation

The Power of PEACE
The stability that brings about momentum

Develop Exponential Power

The Power of PRESENCE
There is no power in being elsewhere

The Power of PURPOSE
The drive behind the goal

The Power of REALITY
Knowing where you are will tell you the directions

The Power of RESPONSIBILITY
Victim or victor, the choice is yours

The Power of TRUST
Opening doors the gentle way

The Power of VISION
How being clear about what you want attracts it

Develop Exponential Power

What's next?

Congratulations! You may have arrived at this page as the last one you'll read. That's great. Or maybe you are someone who, like my wife and uncle, prefers to read the last pages first. Either way here we are, or there you have it: Twenty-seven ways of being with which to generate power so that you can achieve and accomplish things beyond your wildest dreams. You might not be able to integrate all these ways of being into your life all at once and that's completely fine. Don't feel there's something wrong. Instead, give yourself credit for even attempting to go there. Give yourself credit for stretching yourself, for empowering yourself. Take on as many as you're comfortable with. My invitation is to take on four to six at a maximum, maybe even just one at a time, and practice that way of being for as long as it takes until it becomes a habit. You will know when this becomes natural to you.

Then take on another, or another set. Sometimes my wife and I will pick some just for a specific occasion. We may ask each other what we'll need to make a certain event or outcome successful, and we may just choose three or four for the moment or for the day or for a meeting. After the event, we always check and see if we succeeded in being what we had chosen to Be before the event. And it's almost always a match.

Now which one should you choose first? I would choose the ones that most inspire you and those that will have the greatest impact on achieving your goals. So my invitation for you is to choose the ones that will help you achieve success. I call the process "Choosing from the future." Why choose from the future and not the past? Because choosing from the future, choosing what most likely will create that future, will help make it happen with near certainty, and it is what you need to choose and what makes the greatest difference. When I see people choose from the past, when they choose those they are already good at or those that worked in the past, they just create more of the past. I am sure that's not the reason you bought this book.

When you're done with ALL of them, and we're never really done practicing—go right back to the start and practice them all over again. It's an ongoing process and an ongoing journey. The beautiful thing about it is: It's the kind of journey where the process and the experience of traveling counts rather than the destination.

So have fun on your journey and enjoy the trip! I look forward to accompanying you time and again.

Develop Exponential Power

SOME BOOK RECOMMENDATIONS

Recommended reads and other sources of inspiration:

The E-Myth by Michael Gerber

The Celestine Prophecy by James Redfield

Conversations with God – Book 1 to 3, by Neale Donald Walsch

Any books, seminars, and audiobooks by Anthony Robbins

Feel the Fear and do it anyways by Susan Jeffers

The Landmark Forum by Landmark Education Corporation

ABOUT THE AUTHOR

Bjorn C. Martinoff is an Executive Coach working with the world's most senior CEOs and leaders. He is the President of *F1C International,* a company focusing on Executive and Organization Development and which has created turnarounds and accelerated success for several of the world's largest and most famous companies.

He is also the President and founder of *F1CN*, the *Fortune 100 Coaches Network*, and *ODPNi* the *Organization Development Professionals Network International*. Bjorn has worked with the following companies: Samsung, Sony, Mercedes-Benz, Mitsubishi, Nestlé, Unilever, Intel, UBS, Cognizant, Boehringer-Ingelheim, Eli Lilly, NCO, Ovaltine, Twinings, Citigroup, Sanofi Pasteur, Mead Johnson, Zuellig Pharma, Pfizer, Bristol-Myers Squibb, Unilab, Asian Development Bank, Johnson & Johnson, L'Oreal, Avon, IBM, Intel, Maersk Line, Speedo, San Miguel, Nokia, Dell, Logica, One World Connections, Navitaire, Cypress, Sunpower, SGS, Caterpillar, Baker & McKenzie, Pharma Industries, and many others.

Bjorn currently resides in Asia with his wife Victoria (also an Executive Coach) and their four children, Minday, Maxwell, Malcolm, and Sarah.

Develop Exponential Power

Contact Bjorn Martinoff

You can find out more about Bjorn Martinoff and contact him at info@fortune100coach.com or +632-478-3844.

Please also visit the following websites:

www.fortune100coach.com

and

www.f1c-international.com

You can write to us at:

Bjorn Martinoff

c/o F1C International

9719 Pililia Street

Makati City, 1208

Philippines

> There are people who make things happen, there are people who watch things happen, and there are people who wonder what happened. To be successful, you need to be a person who makes things happen.
>
> - *Author unknown*

Develop Exponential Power

www.ingramcontent.com/pod-product-compliance
Lightning Source LLC
Chambersburg PA
CBHW032315230426
43666CB00032B/181